VIEN NA

T0054402

Travel with Marco Polo Insider Tips

MARCO POLO
TOP HIGHLIGHTS

HOFBURG ⭐ 1

The former Habsburg residence is now the President's office, and also home to numerous museums, as well as the national library.

📷 *Tip: It would be hard to find a more beautiful grand hall than the splendid Prunksaal in the Nationalbibliothek.*

➤ p. 36

KUNSTHISTORISCHES MUSEUM (KHM) ⭐

In the KHM you can admire one of the most precious art collections in the world, from paintings by Bruegel to objects in gold.

➤ p. 35

BURGTHEATER ⭐ 3

Both classic and contemporary, provocative performances on one of the most important stages in Europe. The "Burg" is regarded as Austria's national theatre.

➤ p. 110

STEPHANSDOM ⭐

The "Steffl" is Vienna's landmark. As you stroll through the historic city centre, you can't miss the cathedral rising above the roofs (photo).

➤ p. 44

MUSEUMSQUARTIER ⭐ 5

Modern art with Egon Schiele – or just a place to relax? You can do both in this enormous cultural quarter.

📷 *Tip: Use the photo booth to the right of the main entrance for a special selfie.*

➤ p. 51

BELVEDERE ⭐

Want to feel like royalty? This shouldn't be a problem in this Baroque palace on a hilltop, which also houses art galleries.

➤ p. 61

PRATER

A large, popular green space, home to the Giant Ferris Wheel and a main avenue that's more than 4km long!

📷 *Tip: If you love architecture, have a look at the nearby campus of the University of Economics. Its futuristic library, designed by Zaha Hadid, is extremely photogenic.*

➤ p. 58

GLACIS BEISL 8

This central, but nevertheless somewhat hidden, pub serves one of the city's best schnitzels. Its outside space is perfect to escape the summer heat.

➤ p. 80

SCHLOSS SCHÖNBRUNN

Baroque splendour: the magnificent rooms of Maria Theresa's former summer residence and the beautiful and extensive palace park are UNESCO World Heritage Sites.

📷 *Tip: The short climb up to the Gloriette will reward you with fabulous views of Schönbrunn with a Vienna backdrop.*

➤ p. 64

NASCHMARKT 10

Stroll around Vienna's prettiest food market and sample some of the delicacies that are loudly advertised by the traders.

📷 *Tip: If you get up early on Saturday morning, you can take great photos in the busy flea market.*

➤ p. 94

CONTENTS

🕙	Plan your visit	☂	Rainy day activities
€–€€€	Price categories	🐷	Budget activities
		🤹	Family activities
		🚩	Classic experiences

(📖 A2) Refers to the removable pull-out map
(📖 a2) Additional map on the pull-out map
(0) Located off the map

CONTENTS

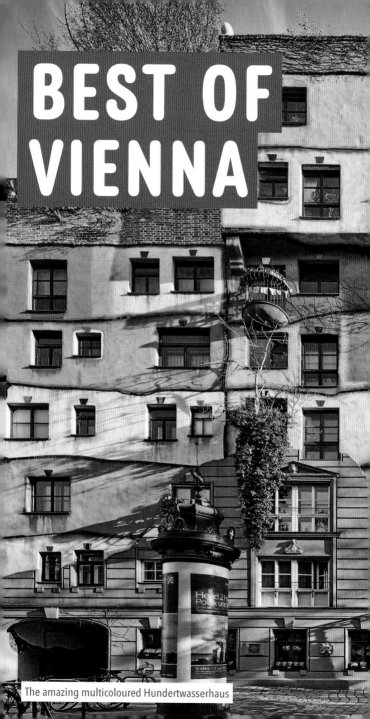

BEST OF
VIENNA

The amazing multicoloured Hundertwasserhaus

BEST WHEN IT RAINS

ACTIVITIES TO BRIGHTEN YOUR DAY

URBAN JUNGLE

It can be raining or freezing outside, but inside *Burggarten*'s *Palmenhaus* (photo), Vienna's oldest Art Nouveau greenhouse, you'll feel like you're in the tropics. Here, you can find colourful butterflies fluttering among palm trees. Make sure you also visit the café for a piece of apple strudel!
➤ p. 34

HOFBURG – AN EXPRESSION OF POWER & GLORY

A tour through the *Imperial Palace*, a vast former epicentre of power, will give you a first-hand impression of how much the Habsburgs loved pomp, as well as their obsession for collecting.
➤ p. 36

WORLD OF MUSIC

If you are expecting a traditional museum, you'll be more than surprised! An extremely entertaining multimedia, interactive journey through the world of music awaits you in the *Haus der Musik* (House of Music), on seven floors in a majestic palace.
➤ p. 42

TIME TRAVEL IN 5D

Ottoman wars, Habsburg monarchs, waltzes and *Sachertorte* – at the *Time Travel Vienna* attraction you can enjoy a high-speed overview of Vienna's proud (and not-so-proud) 2,000-year history with the help of 5D cinema and puppetry.
➤ p. 45

A MUSEUM FOR EVERYBODY

Whether you prefer art, architecture, fashion or dance, you'll find something you like at the *Museumsquartier*, with around 60 cultural attractions. It's in the city centre next to the Mariahilfer Strasse shopping mile.
➤ p. 51

BEST ON A BUDGET

FOR SMALLER WALLETS

SACRED MUSIC

The beautiful *Augustinerkirche* (St Augustin Church) is famous for its solemn masses with music. You can hear festive compositions by Haydn or Schubert performed to a high standard on Sundays and church holidays (admission is free).

➤ p. 34

THE MOST BEAUTIFUL BATHROOM IN VIENNA

Turn a necessity into a pleasure at the *Öffentliche Bedürfnisanstalt am Graben*, a listed Art Nouveau public toilet bedecked with gold and marble. You will feel like you are visiting a museum – but without having to pay an admission fee (just a penny)!

➤ p. 45

SPECTACULAR VIEWS

Of course, the palace and its state rooms are the main attraction, but a walk through the wonderful *Schönbrunn Palace Park* is also a must and, by contrast, free. Don't miss the view over the western part of Vienna from the hilltop *Gloriette* (photo).

➤ p. 65

ESCAPE TO THE ISLAND

The *Donauinsel* is one of the most popular recreation areas in Vienna – mainly because you can play sports, have a barbecue or swim (naked even, if you so choose!), all without paying a penny. During the summer, one of the biggest festivals in the country, the *Donauinselfest*, offers music, theatre and comedy – also free of charge.

➤ p. 67, p.116

VISIT THE OPERA FOR FREE

Mozart, Verdi, Wagner: in summer, the *Filmfestival* projects famous opera and ballet performances onto a big screen on the *Rathausplatz* every evening.

➤ p. 117

BEST WITH CHILDREN

FUN FOR YOUNG & OLD

BEAUTIFUL GREYS!

The *Spanische Hofreitschule* (Spanish Riding School), with its Lipizzaner horses, is an institution. Children can take a tour to see the tack room and visit the greys in their stables (photo).
➤ p. 39

A LOT GOING ON!

The *Museumsquartier* is a children's treasure trove. In the *Zoom Kindermuseum* nobody will be bored, and the *Dschungel-Theater* next door offers attractions for very little ones. The *Museum Moderner Kunst* (Museum of Modern Art) allows kids to get creative.
➤ p. 51

WHO INHABITS THE OCEANS?

Shark-watch or take a walk across the suspension bridge in the adjoining tropical house. More than 10,000 fish and aquatic animals can be found in the *Haus des Meeres* (House of the Ocean).
➤ p. 56

HOW DOES THIS WORK?

How can a plane fly? Where does electricity come from? And how can I build a robot? The *Technisches Museum* allows children to become researchers.
➤ p. 66

STEP ONTO THE WHEEL!

Classic theme park *Böhmischer Prater* is an old-fashioned, homely place with rollercoasters and a Ferris wheel, a few restaurants and nice woodland walks. What more do you need for a family day out?
➤ p. 68

SWING FROM TREE TO TREE!

Test your climbing skills in the *Waldseilpark Kahlenberg* rope park. See how well you can balance at height amid the woods, and swing from tree to tree like Tarzan!
➤ p. 115

BEST ⚑

CLASSIC EXPERIENCES

ONLY IN VIENNA

THE BURGTHEATER – A MUST

The "Burg", as the famous theatre on the Ringstrasse is known, is the city's flagship for German-language theatre. Whether it's for a classic play or a provocatively modern piece, a visit is always worthwhile.

➤ p. 40, p. 110

A TRIP ON THE GIANT FERRIS WHEEL (*RIESENRAD*)

Along with "Steffl" department store and Schloss Schönbrunn, this gigantic steel construction is considered a classic symbol of Vienna. Going for a ride in one of the bright red carriages is a lot of fun, especially in spring when – in the words of the song – "the flowers bloom again in the Prater".

➤ p. 60

DRINK WINE AT A VINEYARD

There are many places in Vienna where you can find a decent glass of wine, but *Neustift am Walde* is one of the most beautiful winegrowing areas surrounding the city, with countless small, family-run *Heurigen* wine taverns nestled among picturesque vineyards.

➤ p. 64

CLASSIC COFFEE HOUSES

Viennese coffee houses are the city's answer to London pubs and Parisian bistros. The hundreds of "public living rooms" throughout the city are still the epitome of everyday Viennese culture. Enjoy the ultimate coffee-house experience at *Café Landtmann* (photo).

➤ p. 75

CHOCOLATE HEAVEN

There is really only one place to taste the original *Sachertorte*, with its two layers of apricot jam, for the first time: *Café Sacher Wien*. Please be aware that, due to the venue's popularity, you may need to queue for a table.

➤ p. 132

GET TO KNOW VIENNA

Shaded by ancient trees: a cool break in the Stadtpark

DISCOVER VIENNA

Vienna is very much a vibrant city, even in the Museumsquartier

There is no city with a higher concentration of clichés per square foot than Vienna. According to the template set by countless kitsch German-language movies, a typical day is roughly as follows: you get up in the morning, drink a *Melange* (a coffee with milk foam) and maybe eat a *Kipferl* (a sort of croissant) with butter and apricot jam, as classical music plays in the background. Your *Fiaker* (traditional horse-drawn carriage) collects you from your home and whisks you away to your workplace, where you unfortunately need to spend a little time, every now and then.

CLICHÉS: FROM THE SCHNITZEL TO THE COFFEE HOUSE

At lunchtime you head off to a *Beisl* (tavern-style) restaurant, where you order (what else?) a schnitzel with potato salad and lamb's lettuce while exchanging

1137
Vienna is mentioned as a city for the first time

1282
Beginning of the Habsburg monarchy, which lasted until the end of World War I

1365
Foundation of the first university (today, Vienna's main university has 90,000 students)

1695
Building work on the Schönbrunn Palace begins

1814
The Congress of Vienna seals Napoleon's defeat and leads to a new European order

earthy, jet-black witticisms with your companions – after all, this is the essence of the legendary *"Wiener Schmäh"*, as Viennese humour is known in the German-speaking world. From here you move on to a coffee house to enjoy a slice of *Sachertorte* or apple strudel with a *Kleiner Brauner* (espresso) – naturally served by a moody waiter wearing a suit that is much too big for him and covered in stains. You then spend the evening enjoying the fine arts – after all, you are in a musical and cultural hotspot.

GLOBAL CITY

So far, so clichéd – and yet there is a kernel of truth to it, as all these things do still exist in reality. Vienna carries the traces of its former role as a global power, as can be seen in the magnificent buildings of the university, the Burgtheater, the opera house and the city's many luxury hotels. And it's as if the monarchy was never completely abolished in the historic heart of the city, where the Habsburg dynasty is kept alive by all possible means, with statues of its most important members on every corner of the Old Town, and thousands of souvenirs of Sisi (Empress Elisabeth) and Emperor Franz Joseph on sale. Vienna continues to stand out as the world capital of high culture, with classical music from the Boys' Choir and Vienna Philharmonic, as well as theatres and major museums.

A GROWING METROPOLIS

Nonetheless, in recent decades the city has ventured a little outside its picture-postcard imperial bubble and developed into a young, vibrant and international

1922
After separating from Lower Austria, Vienna becomes its own federal state

1981
The Donauinsel is opened for recreational use

2008
In the final of the football European Championships in Vienna, Spain defeats Germany 1–0

2015
Sixtieth Eurovision Song Contest held in Vienna (Conchita Wurst having won the previous year)

2026
Vienna's sixth underground line is scheduled to open

metropolis. Today, Vienna is the second biggest city in the German-speaking world – after Berlin. The city is currently home to around 1.9 million people, and over 50 per cent of the city's population has a migrant background.

FOOD DIVERSITY: SACHERTORTE & ĆEVAPČIĆI

The city has been booming for many years now, with the first contribution to diversity made by the Turkish guest workers who came in the 1960s and are raising their children and grandchildren here. During the 1990s they were joined by refugees from the Balkan wars, who stayed on and enriched the city's cultural life with their many clubs and restaurants. As a result, Vienna's cuisine is no longer just *Sachertorte* and schnitzel, but includes dishes such as ćevapčići, kebabs and falafel. Vienna is also characterised by mosques and synagogues; the Jewish quarter growing in the trendy area around the Karmelitermarkt and Taborstrasse offers plenty of kosher shops and small boutiques selling handi-crafts. Meanwhile on Ottakringer Strasse – also known as the Balkan Mile – you can enjoy a *pljeskavica* (meatloaf) at a Croatian restaurant, wash it down with *slivovica* (plum brandy), and then dance to turbo-folk in one of the many clubs.

MORE STUDENTS THAN BERLIN

Austria's accession to the EU in 1995 and the addition of the new eastern member states of Hungary, Slovakia and the Czech Republic attracted a flood of predominantly young people to work and study in Vienna. The city now has the highest student population in the German-speaking world – not least due to the German students who come here to dodge the minimum grade requirements imposed on popular courses of study such as medicine or psychology back at home. Vienna is home to over 200,000 students, and around the universities – whose faculties are scattered across the entire city – there are countless cafés popping up (and in some cases quickly closing down again), where you can find home-made cakes, home-brewed beer and organic slow food. Concept stores selling stylish bikes and clothes are also appearing on every corner in the districts of Neubau and Mariahilf. The youthfulness of Vienna's population is unmistakable in good weather, as students occupy every available inch of the city's parks and green spaces – at least, in locations where this is allowed, as it is forbidden to walk on the grass in many places. They also make their presence felt in the evening, when they put down their books and pack into the city's clubs – which in the last few years have come to include a few genuine gems such as *Grelle Forelle, Fluc* and *Chelsea*.

INSIDER TIP
Browse in hip shops

THE CITY WITH THE HIGHEST QUALITY OF LIFE

Vienna has topped the ranking of cities with the highest quality of life for some years now (according to Mercer's quality of living survey), and naturally the word has got out internationally. Vienna's geographical position as a hub between east and west also makes it attractive to businesses and other organisations, and as a result, over 200 international organisations have moved their headquarters here. Companies operating in life sciences, IT and communications in particular have been moving to Vienna since the millennium. This has given rise to a strong research and development scene – although that's nothing new, as Vienna is where snow globes, waterproof mascara, toothpaste tubes and roller skates were invented. Many of the new companies bring highly qualified international staff with them. The UN has headquarters here (alongside its offices in Geneva, Nairobi and New York City), and it is also home to the EU's Fundamental Rights Agency. The whole world is once again coming to Vienna, and the city is now home to around 25,000 expats.

SOCIAL HOUSING TRADITION

All this means that space in this vibrant city (which is also one of Austria's nine provinces) is becoming increasingly scarce, and the situation is proving difficult to manage, even though the city government is currently building entire new districts. These include the Seestadt Aspern – a mini-metropolis located on open fields in the centre of the city – and the new district of Sonnwendviertel around the main train station. The fact that the city's governing coalition sees the creation of affordable living space as one of its core tasks is a remnant of Vienna's socialist past. Vast workers' residences were built from the 1920s onwards, with examples

You can find many beautiful shops in the Mariahilf quarter

including the Karl-Marx-Hof. This tradition has continued, as the city has been managed by the left-leaning Social Democratic party for decades. Today, over two-thirds of Vienna's inhabitants live in publicly subsidised social housing with low rents, and the city is the largest property owner in Europe. However, this has brought about an explosion in rent charges on the private market, and new arrivals in Vienna – who generally do not have any right to public housing – are forced to shell out a pile of money every month on rent as a result.

SPIES & SECRET AGENTS

Vienna welcomes many short-term visitors on weekend trips, and the city is also well known as a venue for negotiations. It is regularly nominated as one of the best cities in the world for conferences – and since the Cold War it has also been known as a hotbed of espionage. Over 7,000 agents and spies are currently estimated to operate in Vienna – supposedly more than in any other city in the world. This is partly due to a favourable legal context, as espionage is only a crime in Austria when it is directed against Austria itself; as a result, it's completely legal for foreign states to spy on other foreign states in Vienna. Spies are often officially employed in embassies and other international corporations, where they occupy senior roles. However, spying has sometimes led to criminal behaviour, with incidents such as the discovery of the body of a murdered Russian citizen floating in the Danube, or the Kazakh ex-ambassador Rakhat Aliyev being found dead in his prison cell in 2015.

A MORBID STREAK

Melancholy, gloomy and half in love with death – this too is Vienna. Countless Viennese folk songs speak of a bittersweet affection for the Grim Reaper, and

INSIDER TIP
A beautiful corpse

Vienna takes special care of its numerous crypts and catacombs where the Habsburgs and many other guests of honour have their final resting places. There is even a funeral museum documenting Vienna's peculiar interest in death. Balm for the Viennese soul takes the form of a foggy November stroll through one of the many historic cemeteries such as the *Zentralfriedhof* or the bourgeois cemetery of *Sankt Marx*, or through the city centre. Try it out for yourself – it's an interesting blend of the creepy and the peaceful.

DISCOVER YOUR OWN VIENNA

Vienna is not only a young and vibrant place, nor just a preserved, historic city. Vienna is old and young at the same time. It's where monarchy meets modernity. It's both life-affirming and obsessed with the afterlife. It pours old traditions into a cultural melting pot. The city has many faces, from cool and self-confident to shy and inward-looking. Open your heart and your eyes, and Vienna will open itself up to you in turn.

AT A GLANCE

1,935,000
inhabitants

London: 9,648,000

193,000
students

London: 400,000

15km

Höhenstrasse, longest road
Irisgasse, shortest road (17.5m)

365 EUROS

cost of an annual ticket for the
city's public transport network

London: from £1,628

VIENNA'S
RESIDENTS INCLUDE

181

nationalities

SECOND TALLEST
WOODEN BUILDING
IN THE WORLD:

HOHO WIEN

24 FLOORS, LOCATED IN
SEESTADT ASPERN

A POPULAR WORD

OIDA

is what the Viennese say
when they are happy, angry
or surprised, so basically at
any opportunity…

WORLD'S MOST LIVEABLE CITY

based on *The Economist*'s Global Liveability Index 2023
Sydney: 4th place

PRATER

Vienna's biggest park (6km²)

Central Park: 3.41km²

Since 1945, the city's
mayors have been from
SPÖ WIEN

DC TOWER
AUSTRIA'S TALLEST
SKYSCRAPER AT 250M

UNDERSTAND VIENNA

GLAMOUR & SQUALOR

The lives of the Habsburgs provide an inexhaustible treasure trove of anecdotes and absurdities. Take the much-loved Sisi, Empress Elisabeth of Austria and Queen of Hungary, who would nowadays be considered to have mental health issues: she was a cocaine addict (as proven by a syringe on display in the Sisi Museum) and suffered from eating disorders.

However, she was not the only aristocrat to experience an illness of this kind, as Charles V and Maria Theresa both had problems with their relationship with food. By the end of her life, the famous mother of the people was so overweight that she needed a lift to move between floors at Schönbrunn Palace. Although Sisi escaped death by overdose thanks to effective medical care, contemporary sources relate that her distant relative Friedrich III was beyond help: he allegedly overdosed on watermelons, which caused a form of dysentery that resulted in his death.

The life stories of the members of this dynasty, who ruled over Austria for more than six centuries, not only provide material for history books, but would also fill the pages of countless gossip magazines – complete with personalities both great and small, light and darkness, rises and falls, glamour and squalor. All this is part of the reason why Austrians still love the Habsburgs; and there is no question of letting the dead rest in peace. The royal family is always a good subject for a discreet gossip in cafés and bars, and there is a certain degree of seriousness in the way their mythos is kept alive; after all, the city still relies on their legacy in the form of the history and architecture that draw in armies of tourists today.

Incidentally, the Habsburgs are still alive and kicking (although aristocratic titles have been banned in Austria): there are still 500 members of the family out there, around half of whom live in Austria.

CULTURE BATTLE

Rivalled as an iconic Vienna sight only by the Giant Ferris Wheel, *Fiakers* dominate Vienna's cobbled streets. These horse-drawn hackney carriages are encountered everywhere in the city centre, photographed by tourists and pictured on postcards, with smiling drivers in their bowler hats. *Fiakers* have a long tradition: the first *Fiaker* licence in Vienna was granted as early as 1693. At the time there was no law that guaranteed the horses two days' rest per week and five weeks' holiday each year, as is the case today – in line with the law for Austrian citizens. These days, the horses – owned by more than two dozen companies – carry visitors past the Stephansdom and university. However, animal rights activists criticise their daily work in the hot city streets as cruel, and demand its abolition. In 2016, local politicians decided that *Fiakers* were no longer

Anorexic empress: the beautiful Sisi adds charm to all sorts of sweets

allowed to operate above temperatures of 35°C in the shade. This measure didn't ensure the peace: animal rights campaigners continue to protest against *Fiakers*, while the coachmen protest that their livelihood is threatened and say they know best what is good for their animals. This seems like one culture battle that is here to stay.

THE GREAT SCHNITZEL CONSPIRACY

It may come as a shock to you to learn that almost everything you ever thought you knew about Austrian cuisine is a lie. Coffee was not invented in Vienna, but is thought to be a leftover from the Ottoman sieges in the 16th and 17th centuries. And it gets worse: the famous *Wiener Schnitzel* is actually Italian, and originates from 16th-century Venice. Apple strudel and goulash are Hungarian. Desserts such as *Topfengolatschen*, *Powidltascherln*, Mohnnudeln and *Buchteln* come from Bohemia (now in the western Czech Republic), as does the *Serviettenknödel* dumpling that is served as an accompaniment to *Schweinsbraten* roast pork, that most Austrian of dishes. Much of the food served in Vienna was not invented here, but brought together as a kind of highlights reel from the many wars that took place over the preceding centuries. But then again, it doesn't taste any the worse for that.

BOOMTOWN

One of the few areas in which Vienna is not experiencing a shortage in

"Electro swing" pioneer: Parov Stelar has become an international star

capacity is its sewer system. A network of 2,400km of sewers criss-crosses the city, and even if Vienna's current population of 1.9 million people were to double, the system would be able to cope without any difficulty. The credit for this should go to the Habsburgs (who else?), who, in their royal prescience (and mania for grand construction projects), predicted in 1850 that the city would expand to four million inhabitants by 1920, and designed the sewer system accordingly.

The city is still reaping the benefits today, as Vienna is growing at a breakneck pace and its population is hurtling towards the 2 million mark. This growth poses enormous challenges to the city's administrators and politicians, and the Seestadt has become one of Europe's biggest urban development projects. The refugee crisis has also contributed to the population boom, as 80 per cent of all asylum seekers in Austria whose claims are approved move to Vienna. The new arrivals are having an increasing impact on the city's appearance, business life and cuisine. But then again, Vienna has been a multicultural city of immigration for centuries.

AUSTROPOP & WIENERLIED

Once upon a time, there was a globally famous Austropop star named Falco – and then, for a long time after his death in 1998, there was nothing.

Aside from a handful of noteworthy exceptions, the Viennese music industry has produced few internationally successful artists in recent years.

However, the drought is now over, and in the German-speaking world all eyes are on the latest great hopes, Wanda and Bilderbuch, who have reinvented Austropop, are selling out international concert venues, and for the first time in a long while are showing more potential than one-hit wonders such as Eurovision champion Conchita Wurst. The bilingual (German and English) radio station FM4 *(fm4. orf.at)*, which has long acquired cult status, broadcasts a great selection of both local bands and "alternative mainstream", and has helped several artists to attract widespread attention.

INSIDER TIP
We play new Austropop

Alongside Austropop, the traditional *Wienerlied* genre has also been reinterpreted to popular acclaim. Listen out for exponents such as 5/8erl in Ehr'n, Der Nino aus Wien and Voodoo Jürgens. Parov Stelar, a pioneer of "electro swing", even reached the top of the American iTunes Electronic Charts in 2018. And pop musician Mavi Phoenix managed one million hits on YouTube with "Aventura". In addition, hip-hop artists such as Crack Ignaz or Yung Hurn (born in 1995) have become established performers. All in all, the Viennese music scene is currently rejuvenating and reinventing itself, and it's genuinely worth visiting one of the city's clubs to experience this transformation live on stage.

TRUE OR FALSE?

THE GRUMPY VIENNESE

Yes, according to the rankings, the Viennese are supposed to live in the city with the best quality of life in the world, and yet they are still in a bad mood. Motorists moan about cyclists, who in turn are angry with drivers. The neighbours' dogs foul the pavement and other people won't stop asking stupid questions. However, the many rude answers are not meant to be taken that seriously: it's all just *"Wiener schmäh"* (Viennese joking around)! You will meet friendly citizens as well – promise.

CITY OF COFFEE AFICIONADOS

It is true that those who order a *"Kaffee"* while stressing the first syllable give themselves away as not in the know. After all, this word ends in a double "ee". The Viennese have the most creative names for their coffee creations: there is the *Kapuziner* (espresso with a shot of liquid whipped cream), *Einspänner* (espresso with a whipped cream topping) or *Fiaker* (an *Einspänner* with a shot of cherry brandy). However, the days are gone when all locals were able to explain these intricacies. And in hip cafés you will hear more and more often a most non-Viennese order: caffè latte.

PURE WATER FROM THE RAX

Vienna's drinking water comes straight from the mountains, and is guaranteed not to taste of chlorine. Unlike in many other European cities, the tap water here doesn't undergo a purification or chlorination process before it enters people's homes; instead, it is piped directly from the top of a mountain range. This state of affairs is all down to the geologist Eduard Suess. Over 130 years ago, and in the face of considerable opposition, he took the visionary project of constructing a pipeline carrying delicious fresh water from the Rax – a mountain range 90km away – directly into the city, and turned it into a reality. So feel free to drink as much of it as you like – but don't be taken in by the tourist cafés in the 1st District that charge up to five euros for a litre of "Viennese mountain water". Water is generally free, or should cost a maximum of 50 cents per 500ml if you don't order anything else to go with it. And you'll always receive a free glass to go with your food or coffee!

CABARET MEETS COMEDY

Helmut Qualtinger – the forefather of the post-war Viennese cabaret scene and creator of the character of the everyday fascist, Herr Karl – was still alive when satirical cabaret enjoyed its first boom. The predominantly youthful audiences enjoyed the opportunity to drink, smoke and laugh uproariously during performances, while simultaneously believing themselves to be critically minded citizens. Since then, cabaret and stand-up comedy have developed into a mass movement – without compromising on quality. Over a dozen venues now specialise in cabaret, from the small *Niedermair* stage, and the *Orpheum* and *Stadtsaal*, to the *Gloria Theater* and *Gruam* across the Danube.

At the same time, the boundaries between comedy and theatre have become blurred. Stars such as Josef Hader and Thomas Maurer have made a name for themselves as actor-authors staging one-man plays in which they take on a role instead of appearing as themselves. Popular artists also include Michael Niavarani, Viktor Gernot, Alfred Dorfer and Thomas Stipsits. Comedy double act Stermann & Grissemann's talk show *Willkommen Österreich* has been broadcast since 2007 and become a national institution. Comedy duo Maschek, who provide their own, satirical voiceovers for news footage, are also part of the show.

If you speak some German but are concerned that you might not understand the local dialect, then fear not: the majority of performers speak a version of German that is understood by non-Austrians.

WHITE WINE & WILD BOAR

The arch-enemy of wine producers used to be the *phylloxera* aphid; now it's the wild boar. The vineyards around Vienna are the scene of full-on smash-and-grab raids on mild autumn days, as hordes of wild boar gorge on the sweet grapes. The animals are a genuine plague on the 200 winemakers that tend the vines. Despite

Vienna's drinking water originates from the Kläffer spring, high up in the mountains

these incursions, winemakers still manage to produce nearly two million litres of wine each year, four-fifths of which is made up of white wine varieties such as Grüner Veltliner (which always goes down a treat) or Riesling.

INSIDER TIP
Wine instead of water

North of the city, several wine hiking trails allow you to traverse the vineyards *(wein wandern.at/weinwandern-wien)*. You can either turn such a hike into serious exercise, or enjoy the local produce in one of the many wine taverns along the way, known as *Heurigen*. Up until 1456, the wine here was so sour that it would be poured away on the streets of Vienna,

and to prevent any further waste, Emperor Friedrich III decreed that the mortar for the north tower of Stephansdom should be mixed with this nectar of the gods. However, nobody would dream of doing anything like that today, as Viennese wine has since attained international renown. Rainer Christ, Michael Edlmoser and Richard Zahel are just a few examples of winemakers who have won multiple awards. By the way, in Vienna, wine is commonly drunk *"gespritzt"*, or mixed with soda. And if you think this is only done with cheap wines then you'd be wrong. After all, there is never any reason to drink bad wine. Ever.

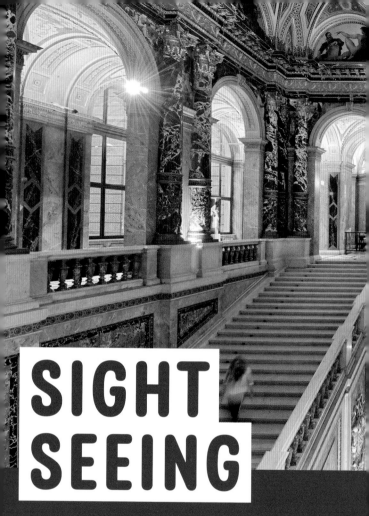

SIGHT SEEING

Vienna is like a cake with a chocolate core: the heart of the city is formed by the medieval centre around which the former suburbs, districts 1 to 9, are grouped like pieces of the cake. Nestled around these are the outer districts 10 to 23.

In the middle of this "city cake", like a single candle, St Stephen's Cathedral reaches into the sky. Around "Steffl", as the cathedral is lovingly known by locals, lies Vienna's historic centre, a UNESCO World Heritage Site and treasure trove of relics that tell the story of centuries of Viennese and European history.

You'll find all the venues in this chapter on the pull-out map 🗺

The opulent Kunsthistorische Museum feels more like a palace

The entire city centre is lined by the Ringstrasse, with Baroque-style and other architectural gems in the form of hotels, opera houses, theatres and university buildings. Here you can see, feel and understand how the world was once governed from Vienna – after all, the great rulers of the Habsburg dynasty are buried in this part of the city. With its many churches, historic squares and apartment buildings, the 1st District is an open-air museum that is best explored on foot.

OVERVIEW OF CITY NEIGHBOURHOODS

Neustift am Walde ★

MARCO POLO HIGHLIGHTS

★ **RINGSTRASSE**
Parade of late-19th-century
monumental architecture on Vienna's
showcase boulevard ➤ p. 30

★ **KUNSTHISTORISCHES MUSEUM**
Magnificent building on the Ringstrasse
with countless masterpieces by Titian,
Bruegel, Rembrandt and so on ➤ p. 35

★ **HOFBURG**
The heart of the empire ➤ p. 36

★ **KAISERLICHE SCHATZKAMMER**
Priceless Habsburg heirlooms ➤ p. 38

★ **STEPHANSDOM**
Vienna's Gothic cathedral ➤ p.44

★ **MUSEUMSQUARTIER**
Vienna's culture quarter with more than
20 museums ➤ p.51

★ **PRATER**
Green oasis for fun and sport ➤ p. 58

★ **BELVEDERE**
Prince Eugene's fairytale palace ➤ p.61

★ **HEERESGESCHICHTLICHES MUSEUM**
War in the museum, where it belongs
➤ p. 62

★ **NEUSTIFT AM WALDE**
Hospitable *heurigen* wine taverns in a
village of vineyards ➤ p.64

★ **SCHLOSS SCHÖNBRUNN**
The Habsburgs' charming residence
➤ p. 64

NEUBAU, JOSEFSTADT & ALSERGRUND p. 50

Art, culture,
design – here is where
the young Vienna
works and shops

THE CENTRE (WEST) p. 30

Breathe the history of
monarchy: Hofburg,
Parliament, Rathaus

Hofburg ★ ⦿
Kaiserliche Schatzkammer ★ ⦿
Ringstrasse ★ ⦿
Kunsthistorisches Museum ★ ⦿
Museumsquartier ★ ⦿

MARIAHILF, MARGARETE & WIEDEN p. 55

Hip Vienna
at and around the
Naschmarkt and
Mariahilfer Strasse

Auer-Welsbach-
Park

⦿ Schloss Schönbrunn ★

Schönbrunner
Schlosspark

LEOPOLDSTADT & LANDSTRASSE p. 58

Jewish community, joggers in the Prater and a Baroque palace

THE CENTRE (EAST) p. 42

Historic centre with the imposing Stephansdom

Floridsdorfer Brücke

A22

Brigittenauer Brücke

Donaupark

Arbeiterstrandbadstraße

Wagramer Straße

Reichsbrücke

A22

Augarten

Nordbahnstraße

Taborstraße

Handelskai

Prater

Donaukanal

Untere Donaustraße

Weißgerberlände

Stephansdom

Park Prater

Parkring

Stadtpark

Schüttelstraße

Erdberger Lände

A23

Ungargasse

Landstraßer Hauptstraße

Belvedere-garten

Rennweg

Belvedere

Schlachthausgasse

Baumgasse

Erdbergstraße

A4

Landstraßer Gürtel

Schweizergarten

Heeresgeschichtliches Museum

A23

750 m
820 yd

Visitors in search of more variety can make a detour across the Donaukanal (Danube canal) into the 2nd District of Leopoldstadt, which is the centre of Vienna's Jewish life, as well as being home to one of the biggest theme parks in Europe and one of the city's biggest green spaces in the form of the Prater. The 6th and 7th districts, extending on either side of the Mariahilfer Strasse shopping street, are where things get young and hip, and the side streets here have in recent years become home to a whole host of trendy cafés and bars, along with designers, contemporary artists and photographers hard at work in their studios. The driving force behind this development is undoubtedly the Museumsquartier, which serves as a focal point for contemporary art. The

middle-class districts of Josefstadt and Alsergrund (8th and 9th) are somewhat quieter and more dignified, and are home to theatres, dainty villas and bourgeois buildings. At any rate, you can't discover Vienna by sticking to the central districts, so it's worth venturing a little further afield, too. And don't worry if you get lost – on every street sign there is a number next to the name of the road that tells you which district you are in.

THE CENTRE (WEST)

Due to its sheer volume of tourist attractions, we have split the centre of Vienna into two sections. The – admittedly rather artificial – dividing line between the western and eastern parts of the city is the arrow-straight line of streets that links Schottentor to the Staatsoper.

The main attractions in this half of "the first" (as the historic heart of the city is known by locals) are the Hofburg and the western section of the Ringstrasse, with its many prestigious buildings.

■ RINGSTRASSE ★ ⚑

After Emperor Franz Joseph had ordered that Vienna's old defensive walls be torn down in 1857, he had a splendid boulevard created to take their place. It circles the historical city centre and meets the Danube Canal at two places on Franz-Josefs-Kai. This

Has cycling with no hands on the Ringstrasse been approved by Parliament?

4.5km-long ring road is lined by numerous majestic private and public buildings in eclectic, historicist style – sometimes known as Ringstrasse Style – incorporating classical, Gothic, Renaissance and Baroque elements. A work of art in its entirety, the "Ring" was opened in 1865. No other European metropolis has anything to match it. Pedestrians have to share certain sections of the Ringstrasse with cyclists. ▯ a–d 6–8

2 SECESSION

In the words of the architect Josef Maria Olbrich, his creation was intended to be "white and gleaming, holy and chaste". In 1897/98, he created this exhibition and club building for the Viennese Secession, a group of avant-garde artists who split from their conservative colleagues. The latter had their headquarters in the Künstlerhaus. The Secession building, with a dome of filigree, gold-plated foliage is one of the principal works of Viennese Art Nouveau. Incidentally, the contents of the building are any-thing but chaste, as time and again its changing exhibition programme returns to erotic themes. *Tue–Sun 10am–6pm | admission 9.50 euros for exhibitions | Friedrichstr. 12 | secession. at | U1, U2, U4 Karlsplatz |* ▯ *b8*

3 AKADEMIE DER BILDENDEN KÜNSTE ☂

The Academy of Fine Arts, in the style of the High Renaissance, is decorated with terracotta and frescoes and is home to the world-famous picture gallery with a representative selection

THE CENTRE (WEST)

27 Votivkirche

Ostarrichi-Park

Sigmund-Freud-Park

Maria-Theresien Str.

Schottenring

Universitätsstr.

ring

Wipplingerstraße

Landesgerichtstraße

Universität **25**

26 Beethoven Pasqualatihaus

23 Wien Museum MUSA

22 Wiener Rathaus

24 Burgtheater

Rathaus-park

Rathauspl.

Universitätsring

Stadiongasse

19 Minoritenkirche

Stephans-platz

Auerspergstr.

Parlament **21**

Silberkammer **17** **18** Loooshaus

Kaiserappartements **17** **14** Hofburg ★

Volksgarten **20**

Sisi Museum **17** **16** Spanische Hofreitschule

Schmerlingplatz

Museumstr.

15 Kaiserliche Schatzkammer ★

Neustiftgasse

Bellariastraße

12 Heldenplatz

8 Augustinerkirche

11 Naturhistorisches Museum

Theatermuseum **5**

Mahnmal gegen
7 Krieg und Faschismus

1 Ringstrasse ★

6 Albertina &
Albertina Modern

Weltmuseum Wien **13**

Burggarten **9**

Museums-platz

10 Kunsthistorisches Museum ★

Opernring

4 Staatsoper

Getreidemarkt

Kärntner Ring

Gumpendorfer Str.

3 Akademie der Bildenden Künste

Friedrichstr.

Karlsplatz

2 Secession

Resselpark

250 m
273 yd

---

of Western art from six centuries. Hans Baldung Grien, Lucas Cranach the Elder, Titian, Sandro Botticelli, Peter Paul Rubens, Rembrandt and Anthony van Dyck are just some of the masters whose works are on display here. The absolute highlight of the collection is the triptych *The Last Judgement* by Hieronymus Bosch, a magnificent display of fascinating, but cruel, phantasmagorical scenes. The associated *Kupferstichkabinett* (Cabinet of Prints and Drawings) has several hundred pictures from the Biedermeier period, as well as medieval architectural drawings. *Tue–Sun 10am–6pm | admission 9 euros | Schillerplatz 3 | akademiegalerie.at | tram 1, 2, 71, D, bus 57A Burgring | U1, U2, U4 Karlsplatz |* ⊞ *b8*

4 STAATSOPER

The Imperial and Royal Opera House, with its loggia, arcades on the side and metal barrel roof, was subjected to massive criticism when inaugurated in 1869. Since then, the Viennese have come to admire the neo-Renaissance-style building, which was severely damaged in the final weeks of World War II, and consider it one of the main symbols of the city's musical culture. The interior, with its frescoed staircase, Schwind Foyer, Gustav Mahler and Marble Halls, and auditorium accommodating 2,276, can be visited on a guided tour *(times at the side entrance, online or tel. 01 5 14 44 26 13). Opernring 2 | wiener-staatsoper.at | tram D, 1, 2, 71, bus 59A, U1, U2, U4 Karlsplatz/Oper | ▥ b7*

5 THEATERMUSEUM

Its 1.5 million objects make the Austrian Theatre Museum in the magnificent Palais Lobkowitz the largest of its kind in the world. There are also regular special exhibitions in its splendid Baroque halls; furthermore, the collection of the former State Opera Museum is on show here. *Wed–Mon 10am–6pm (tours by appointment) | tel. 01 5 25 24 27 29 | admission 12 euros | Lobkowitzplatz 2 | theatermuseum.at | U1, U2, U4 Karlsplatz/ Oper | ◷ 30–60 mins | ▥ b7*

6 ALBERTINA & ALBERTINA MODERN

The Palais Albertina, located diagonally behind the State Opera, has the world's largest collection of graphic art. It contains 60,000 drawings and

Franz Joseph on horseback, as viewed from the "flying" roof of the Albertina

watercolours as well as around 1.5 million prints from almost all of the artists active in the past 600 years. Their sensitivity to light makes it impossible to show them permanently. Some 500 works of classic modern art from the Batliner Collection are on display in the painstakingly renovated building and temporary exhibitions with works by the greatest masters are held regularly. A second site, the Albertina Modern, displays modern and contemporary art. *Sat–Tue, Thu, 10am–6pm, Wed, Fri 10am–9pm | admission Albertina 17.90 euros, Albertina Modern 14.90 euros, combined ticket 24.90 euros | Albertinaplatz 1 | albertina.at | tram D, 1, 2, 62, 65, 71, bus 2A, U 1, 2, 4 Karlsplatz/Oper | ◷ 1 hr | ▥ b7*

7 MAHNMAL GEGEN KRIEG UND FASCHISMUS

Since the 1980s, a monument by Alfred Hrdlicka on the square behind the Opera House keeps alive the memory of victims of World War II and Nazi dictatorship in Austria between 1938 and 1945. The group of sculptures incorporates the two-part, granite *Gates of Violence*, the bronze figure of the *Kneeling Jew* and the marble statue *Orpheus entering Hades*. The declaration of independence of the Second Republic of 27 April 1945, is cited on a stele. *Albertinaplatz/Augustinerstr.* | *bus 3A, U1, U2, U4 Karlsplatz* | ▥ *b7*

8 AUGUSTINERKIRCHE

First-rate performances of 🐷 sacred music, free of charge, every Sunday at 11am in the beautiful Gothic church of St Augustine, with its sandstone high altar. *Augustinerstr. 3* | *augustinerkirche.at* | *tram D, 1, 2, bus 2A, U1, U2, U4 Karlsplatz* | ▥ *b7*

9 BURGGARTEN

Laid out for the exclusive use of the imperial family in 1818, the garden behind the National Library near the Hofburg opened its gates to the public 100 years later. When the sun is shining you will find students learning or lounging on the lawns, while the Lipizzaner horses from the Spanish Riding School are taken for their morning walks here. The park's 🐷 *Palmenhaus* is one of the most beautiful Art Nouveau greenhouses in Vienna, and also features a café with a large terrace that serves superb food (*Mon–Thu 10am–11pm, Fri 10am–midnight, Sat 9am–midnight, Sun 9am–10pm*). Up to 500 butterflies inhabit the neighbouring glasshouse

The brasserie in the Burggarten's palm house is a pleasant place to eat

(April–Oct Wed–Fri 10am–5pm, Sat/ Sun until 6.30pm, Nov–March daily 10am–4pm | admission 7 euros). Burgring/Opernring | tram D, 1, 2, bus 57A | ⊞ b7

🔟 KUNSTHISTORISCHES MUSEUM ★ 👶

The Kunsthistorische (KHM), designed by the Ringstrasse architects Gottfried Semper and Karl von Hasenauer, is one of the world's largest art museums. Its holdings are the result of the collecting passion of Habsburg monarchs who, starting in the 16th century, systematically amassed precious objects. The main attraction is the painting gallery on the first floor. It is the fourth largest of its kind in the world. Its treasures include many major works by Bruegel, Rubens, Rembrandt, Dürer, Raphael, Titian, Tintoretto, Veronese, Caravaggio, Velázquez and other masters of the Italian, French, Spanish and Dutch/ Flemish schools from the late 15th to 17th centuries. The collection's second focal point is the Kunstkammer (Collection of Sculpture and Decorative Arts), with priceless gold pieces like the famous *Saliera* by Benvenuto Cellini, carved stones and ivory, automatons, clocks, astrological instruments and much more. The magnificent paintings on the ceilings and walls by Ernst and Gustav Klimt, Michael Munkácsy, Hans Makart and others are also well worth seeing.

The magnificent building, opened at the end of the 19th century, also houses a coin cabinet and the Egyptian and Near Eastern Collection, as well as a collection of Greek and Roman antiquities. On Thursday evening, an opulent buffet is served in the domed hall. The Collection of Ancient Musical Instruments, the Collection of Arms and Armour, as well as the *Ephesus Museum*, can be visited in the Neue Burg on the other side of the Ringstrasse. The KHM offers a special programme and free guided tours for children. Even those who don't care much for art may be convinced otherwise by the half-hour lunchtime tours *(Tue, Thu 12.30pm | 3 euros)*. *Fri–Wed 10am–6pm, Thu 10am–9pm | admission 18 euros | Burgring 5 | entrance Maria-Theresien-Platz | khm.at | tram D, 1, bus 57A, U2 Museumsquartier | U2, U3 Volkstheater | ⏱ from 2 hrs | ⊞ a7–8*

INSIDER TIP
Art instead of Knödel

🔟 NATURHISTORISCHES MUSEUM

If it weren't for the little elephant guarding the entrance, you wouldn't know where you were. The Museum of Natural History lies directly opposite the Kunsthistorische Museum – and looks just the same from the outside. However, inside you won't find any Old Masters, but dinosaur skeletons, the Venus of Willendorf – a 26,000-year-old stone statuette, loads of stuffed animals and the world's largest collection of insects, with more than six million specimens. An additional attraction: tours of the roof with a great view over the historic buildings of the 1st District. *Thu–Mon 9am–6.30pm, Wed 9am–9pm |*

admission 14 euros | roof tours Wed 6.30pm, Sun 4pm | admission 9 euros | info tel. 01 52 17 70 | Burgring 7 | entrance Maria-Theresien-Platz | nhm-wien.ac.at | tram D, 1, 2, 46, 49, bus 48A, U2, U3 Volkstheater | ⏱ from 2 hrs | 🔲 a7

12 HELDENPLATZ

Prince Eugene's steed rears up aggressively, while Archduke Charles sits on horseback opposite him. Together, these two generals watch over Heldenplatz – which by night is one of the most impressive spots in all Vienna, with its views of the beautifully illuminated Hofburg, multiple museums, the Rathaus and the Parliament building. Just a few metres away from the two generals, on neighbouring Ballhausplatz, you can find the memorial to deserters who fell victim to the Nazi military justice system during the war. *Heldenplatz | tram D, 1, 2, 71, bus 2A, U3 Herrengasse | 🔲 a7*

13 WELTMUSEUM WIEN

Vienna's Museum of Ethnography is one of the most comprehensive in Europe. The main highlights are James Cook's collection from Oceania, bronze sculptures from Benin and Mexican treasures including the famous Feather Crown of Montezuma. There are also fascinating temporary exhibitions focusing on one subject. *Thu-Mon 10am-6pm, Tue 10am-9pm | admission 16 euros | Neue Burg | Heldenplatz | weltmuseumwien.at | tram 1, 2, 71, D, bus 57A Burgring | U2, U3 Volkstheater | ⏱ 1–2 hrs | 🔲 b7*

14 HOFBURG ★ 🚩 🎭

For more than 600 years – from when Habsburg King Rudolf I received feudal rights to the lands of Austria (1276) until the abdication of Emperor Karl (1918) – the Imperial Palace (the "Burg") was the residence of the Austrian dynasty. Initially a comparatively small castle, it increased in size over the centuries in keeping with the power and extent of its residents' empire, to become the labyrinthine complex of buildings with 18 wings and 19 courtyards that exists today.

The *Schweizerhof* is the oldest section. Here, one can enter the *Kaiserliche Schatzkammer* (Imperial Treasury) and *Burgkapelle* (Court Chapel), whose core is Gothic. The *Stallburg*, *Amalientrakt* (Amalie's

Wing), and the red, black and gold *Schweizertor* (Swiss Gate) at the entrance to the court of the same name were created in the 16th century. The *Leopoldinische Trakt* (Leopold's Wing) was added in the 17th century, followed in the 18th by the *Reichskanzleitrakt* (Imperial Chancellor's Wing), built under the direction of Johann Lukas von Hildebrandt and Joseph Emanuel Fischer von Erlach. Father and son Fischer von Erlach also created the *Winterreitschule*, where the Lipizzaner horses of the Spanish Riding School perform, as well as the *National-bibliothek*. Many consider the building, with its Baroque *Prunksaal* (State Hall) featuring an enormous dome, the world's most beautiful library. The *Michaelertrakt* was completed at the end of the 19th century. And finally, the *Neue Burg* wing was built between 1891 and 1913 as part of a major expansion project that was not completed because of World War I.

Only a tiny portion of the approximately 2,500 rooms in this labyrinth of stone can be visited. These include the *Kaiserappartements* (Imperial Apartments) with the Sisi Museum as well as the *Silberkammer* (Silver Collection). Both are accessible from the domed room in the *Michaelertrakt*. Also accessible are the *Kaiserliche Schatzkammer*, the *Burgkapelle*, the *Prunksaal* (State Hall) in the *Nationalbibliothek* (Tue/Wed, Fri–Sun 10am–6pm, Thu 10am–9pm | admission 8 euros | Josefsplatz 1 | onb.ac.at),

The Hofburg is a dizzying megacomplex of 2,500 rooms

A sea of red roses in summer: the Volksgarten beside the Hofburg

the Spanish Riding School, the *Hofjagd und Rüstkammer* (Collection of Arms and Armour), the collection of ancient musical instruments, the *Weltmuseum Wien* (House of Austrian History) and the Ephesus Museum. *Various tickets from 16 euros | Michaelerplatz 1, Josefsplatz, Heldenplatz, Ballhausplatz | hofburg-wien.at | tram D, 1, 2, 71, bus 2A Burgring | U1, U2, U4 Karlsplatz | ☉ 4–6 hrs | ▥ b7*

⓯ KAISERLICHE SCHATZKAMMER ★

The Imperial Treasury, one of the world's most valuable collections of religious and secular artefacts, is located in the oldest section of the Hofburg, the *Schweizerhof*. You will be dazzled by the priceless coronation regalia, insignia from orders of chivalry, national emblems, jewellery and mementos displayed in the 20 rooms. The imperial regalia and relics of the Holy Roman Empire are among the most precious objects. These include the orb and sword, sceptre, the legendary holy lance that supposedly pierced the breast of Jesus Christ, as well as the Crown of the Reich, created in 962 CE, making it the oldest of its kind in the world. The treasure that Maria of Burgundy brought into her marriage with the later Emperor Maximilian I in 1477 is similarly precious, as are objects of the Order of the Golden Fleece. Many weird and wonderful items can be seen in Ferdinand I's *Kunstkammer* (Cabinet of Curiosities). *Wed–Mon 9am–5.30pm | admission 14 euros | Hofburg/*

Schweizerhof | kaiserliche-schatz kammer.at | tram D, 1, 2, 71, bus 1A, 2A, 57A Burgring | ⏱ *1–2 hrs |* ⎕ *b7*

16 SPANISCHE HOFREITSCHULE 🎭

If you hear a whinny and catch a whiff of horse manure coming from the building that houses Austria's president, don't worry, you aren't hallucinating. The Hofburg is also home to the Spanish Riding School, with its Lipizzaner stallions. You can watch the white horses at morning training or in performance. Tickets, including those for tours that take in a visit to the stables lasting around an hour, are available at the visitors' centre at Michaelerplatz 1 or online at *srs.at (daily 9am–4pm | tickets from 14 euros, guided tour from 19 euros, shows from 27 euros, children 3–6 free, 6–12 concession). Schedules tel. 01 5 33 90 31 |* ⎕ *b7*

17 KAISERAPPARTEMENTS, SILBERKAMMER & SISI MUSEUM

This is how dinner was served at the Viennese court: on fine china from East Asia, Sèvres and Augarten, with crystal glasses and silver cutlery. The highlight of the *Silberkammer* is the almost 30m-long Milanese table centre-piece and a state dining service for 140 people. The *Imperial Apartments* include the private rooms of Emperor Franz Joseph I and his wife Elisabeth, their dining room, audience hall and the quarters of the imperial officers' corps. The *Sisi Museum* is also part of this complex and shows the "truth and not the myth" about

Empress Elisabeth, alias Sisi, who has been transfigured into something of a legend. *Daily 9am–5.30pm, last admission 4.30pm | admission 16 euros for Kaiserappartements, Silberkammer and Sisi Museum | Sisi Ticket – Sisi Museum with Schönbrunn, Hofburg and Imperial Furniture Collection 40 euros | Innerer Burghof, Kaisertor | sisimuseum-hofburg.at | bus 2A, U1 Herrengasse |* ⏱ *1–2 hrs |* ⎕ *b7*

18 LOOSHAUS

No other architectural project in Vienna caused as much controversy as this residential and commercial building built by Adolf Loos in 1911. The bold design, with an elegant, unadorned exterior of green marble and glass, is a landmark on the path to the functional building style of the 20th century. *Michaelerplatz 3 | bus 2A, 3A | U3 Herrengasse |* ⎕ *b6*

19 MINORITENKIRCHE

The three-naved Church of the Friars Minor, with ridge turrets typical of the mendicant order, was built in the Gothic period (14th century). The elaborate tracery of the windows and portal, the mosaic of the Last Supper – a copy of Leonardo da Vinci's fresco – are outstanding. *Minoritenplatz | U3 Herrengasse |* ⎕ *b6*

20 VOLKSGARTEN

After Napoleon had had the castle bastions torn down in 1908, a park with a strictly geometric layout was laid out "for the people" on the space created. Peter Nobile erected the

Theseus Temple in the middle of the complex. The rose garden near the exit to the Burgtheater is famous for its splendid blossoms. *Tram D, 1, 2, 71 Parlament, U2, U3 Volkstheater | ▥ a–b 6–7*

21 PARLAMENT 🐷

The Parliament building, erected between 1873 and 1883, is the seat of both the National and Federal Councils. The architect, Theophil Hansen, wanted the Greek ideals of democracy to be preserved through his choice of a classical style and the statue of the goddess of wisdom, Athena, in front of the main entrance. The building has been extensively renovated, with work completed at the end of 2022. For current guided tour information please visit the website. *Admission free | booking for groups required: tel. 01 4 01 10 24 00 | Dr Karl Renner-Ring 3 | parlament. gv.at | tram D, 1, 2, 71 Parlament | U 2, 3 Volkstheater | ⏱ 1 hr | ▥ a7*

22 WIENER RATHAUS

The splendid neo-Gothic New Town Hall was constructed in 1872/73. This is where the lord mayor and the municipal and provincial governmental authorities have their offices. The interior – the arcaded courtyard, ceremonial staircase and enormous ceremonial hall – can be visited on a guided tour. The 6m-high *Rathausmann* (Town Hall Man), a kind of gigantic iron mascot holding a standard, watches over the city from the top of the almost 100m-high tower. In summer, films of operas and concerts are shown on an enormous screen in front of the main façade, with its loggias, balconies and narrow lancet windows. There are also many monuments in the *Rathauspark. Free guided tours Mon, Wed, Fri 1pm (except when in session or during holidays) | Friedrich-Schmidt-Platz 1 | tram D, 1, 71 Rathausplatz | tram 2, U2 Rathaus | ▥ a6*

23 WIEN MUSEUM MUSA

The MUSA, next to the Rathaus, exhibits mainly contemporary Viennese art in its 600-m² space. It is part of the Wien Museum, which is the city's cultural archive. Until the main site at the Karlsplatz has been renovated, the MUSA will host changing exhibitions about the city's historical, cultural or long-forgotten points of interest. 🐷 Admission is free for under-19s, and everyone else can get in free on the first Sunday of each month. *Tue–Sun 10am–6pm | admission 7 euros, free under-19s | Felderstrasse 6–8 | musa. at (information on the renovation at wienmuseumneu.at) | tram D, 1, 71 Rathausplatz | tram 2, U2 Rathaus | ⏱ 1–2 hrs | ▥ J7–8*

24 BURGTHEATER ⚑

It's not only what happens on stage that makes this temple of German thespian culture interesting. The building itself is well worth a visit. It was built between 1874 and 1888 to plans by Gottfried Semper and Carl von Hasenauer, with a façade in the style of the Italian High Renaissance, colossal busts of great poets over the windows and a spectacular interior with ceremonial staircases, refreshment rooms and seating for 1,500. *Guided tours (approx. 1 hr) Thu/Fri 3pm, Sat/Sun 11am, Aug Mon–Fri 3pm | admission 8 euros | Universitätsring 2 | burgtheater.at | tram D, 1, 37, 38, 40–44, 71, U2 Schottentor | ▦ a6*

25 UNIVERSITÄT

The main building of the University of Vienna, which was founded in 1365, is one of the most spectacular buildings on the Ringstrasse. It was built in neo-Renaissance style to plans drawn up by Heinrich Ferstel in the 1870s and in addition to guided tours, it can be toured with the *Uni Wien Guides* app. The highlight of the tour through the auditorium and lecture halls is the series of busts of 154 famous scientists in the arcaded courtyard. *Guided tours Thu 6pm, Sat 10.30am |*

admission 5 euros | Universitätsring 1 | event.univie.ac.at | tram D, 1, 37, 38, 40–44, 71, U2 Schottentor | ☉ 30–60 mins | ▦ a6

26 PASQUALATIHAUS

Ludwig van Beethoven moved house about 60 times within Vienna and surroundings. One of the best-known addresses is the classical-style Pasqualati House, where he composed, among other things, his opera *Leonore*, which later became known as *Fidelio*. While Beethoven's flat itself cannot be viewed, a small museum with manuscripts and audio stations has been created in a neighbouring apartment on the fourth floor (no lift available). *Tue–Sun 10am–1pm, 2–6pm | admission 5 euros | Mölker Bastei 8 | wienmuseum.at | tram D, 1, 37, 38, 40–44, 71, bus 1A, U2 Schottentor | ☉ 30–45 mins | ▦ a6*

The Rathaus tower keeps an eye on the goings-on in Parliament

27 VOTIVKIRCHE

The Votivkirche, consecrated in 1879, is one of the pre-eminent sacred buildings in Vienna and at 99m high, it's the city's second tallest church, only topped by the Stephansdom. The freely accessible, albeit dark, basilica includes eight side chapels and features impressive ceiling chandeliers. The original stained-glass windows were destroyed in World War II and recreated afterwards. At the time of writing, the church was still under restoration, so parts of its frontal façade are unfortunately covered by a big advertising board. *Tue–Sat 11am–7pm, Sun 9am–1pm | admission free | guided tours every last Sat of the month at 2pm (booking tel. 0664 5 2 1 07 50 | 17 euros | Rooseveltplatz 8 | votivkirche.at | tram D, 1, 37, 38, 4–44, 71, U2 Schottentor |* 🗺 *a5*

THE CENTRE (EAST)

To the east of the Hofburg and Freyung lies Vienna's warren of medieval alleyways, with Stephansdom towering above them all. The historic buildings here have been restored to an extremely high standard and more than ever before are filled with vibrant life.

This dynamism is generated by elegant shops and a booming bar scene, as well as a number of cultural initiatives and countless superb museums.

28 HAUS DER MUSIK ☂

Visitors take an interactive multimedia journey through the world of sound – from the Vienna Philharmonic Orchestra, which was founded here in 1842, to computer-controlled hyper-instruments that can be experimented with – on the seven floors of this carefully renovated palace. *Daily 10am–10pm | admission 16 euros | Seilerstätte 30 | hdm.at | tram D, 2, 71 Schwarzenbergplatz | U1, U2, U4 Karlsplatz |* ⏱ *1–2 hrs |* 🗺 *c7*

29 KAPUZINERGRUFT

Since 1632, all Habsburg rulers and their closest relatives have been buried here in the Imperial Crypt underneath the Capuchin Church, although their hearts have found their final resting place in St Augustin's Church and their internal organs in the catacombs of St Stephen's. The last emperor to be interred here was Franz Joseph I in 1916. The last burial of a crowned head, however, took place in 1989 when Empress Zita, Karl I's widow, was laid to rest here. The most magnificent of the 138 metal coffins is the double sarcophagus Balthasar Ferdinand Moll created for Maria Theresa and her husband Franz I Stephan of Lorraine. You may think that visiting sarcophaguses is macabre. 🐟 **INSIDER TIP** **Hello Goths!** However, many children find it fascinating, and there is a 75-minute guided tour including a quiz for 7- to 13-year-olds at least once a month. Online booking required. *Daily 10am–6pm | admission 8 euros | Neuer Markt 2*

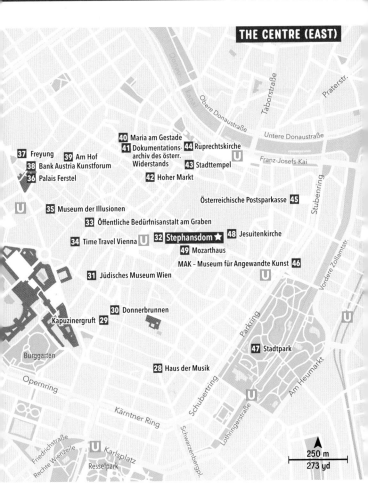

THE CENTRE (EAST)

40 Maria am Gestade
41 Dokumentations-archiv des österr. Widerstands
44 Ruprechtskirche
37 Freyung
39 Am Hof
38 Bank Austria Kunstforum
43 Stadttempel
36 Palais Ferstel
42 Hoher Markt
Österreichische Postsparkasse 45
35 Museum der Illusionen
33 Öffentliche Bedürfnisanstalt am Graben
34 Time Travel Vienna
32 Stephansdom ★
48 Jesuitenkirche
49 Mozarthaus
MAK – Museum für Angewandte Kunst 46
31 Jüdisches Museum Wien
30 Donnerbrunnen
Kapuzinergruft 29
47 Stadtpark
Burggarten
28 Haus der Musik
Opernring
Kärntner Ring
250 m
273 yd

| kapuzinergruft.com | bus 3A, U1, U3 Stephansplatz | ⏱ 1 hr | ▥ c7

30 DONNERBRUNNEN

Vienna's most beautiful fountain, also known as the Providentiabrunnen, was created between 1737 and 1739 – a masterpiece by the great Baroque sculptor Georg Raphael Donner. The statue in the centre shows Prudence, the allegory of caution. The figures around the edge of the pool personify the four main tributaries of the Danube in Austria – the Traun, Enns, Ybbs and March rivers. Donner's lead sculptures were replaced by bronze copies in the 19th century; the originals are in the Baroque Museum in the Lower Belvedere. *Neuer Markt* | bus 2A, U1, U3 Stephansplatz | ▥ c7

Find heavenly peace in St Stephen's – although it's rarely as empty as this!

31 JÜDISCHES MUSEUM WIEN

A permanent exhibition of Jewish religious history and suffering, as well as temporary shows dealing with Jewish literature, architecture, photography, and so on. It's also worthwhile continuing on to Judenplatz, where Rachel Whiteread's cube-shaped monument commemorates the Shoah and an extension to the museum in the *Misrachi House (□ b7)* documents community life during the Middle Ages and displays the archaeological remains of a synagogue. *Sun–Fri 10am–6pm | admission 12 euros (combined ticket with Misrachi-Haus) | Dorotheergasse 11 | jmw.at | U1, U3 Stephansplatz | ⏱ 1–2 hrs | □ b-c7*

32 STEPHANSDOM ⭐ 🚩

St Stephen's Cathedral, which the Viennese lovingly call "Steffl", is one of the city's main landmarks and Austria's most important example of Gothic architecture. Its history can be traced back to 1147, when the first Romanesque church was consecrated here. This was replaced in the middle of the 13th century by another Romanesque building whose remains – the Giant's Door (Riesentor) and two Heathen Towers (Heidentürme) – still form the western front of the cathedral.

The building as we know it today was created in several stages: 1303–40, the three-naved Albertine Choir; starting in 1359, the main nave with its magnificent stellar and net-rib-vaulted ceilings, as well as the 137m-high South Tower. Its planned companion piece, the North Tower, was never completed and was adorned with a small, Renaissance-style dome in 1579. The Pummerin, a 21-ton bell made from the metal of cannons captured during the second Turkish siege (1683), now hangs there.

The interior of the cathedral, which the architect Adolf Loos described as the "most solemn on earth", houses numerous unique artistic treasures. The most important are the pulpit made by Anton Pilgram in 1514-15, the Gothic Wiener Neustadt Altar from 1447, the cenotaph of Emperor Friedrich III, which Niclas Gerhaert van Leyden worked on from 1467-1513, and the tomb of Prince Eugene of Savoy from 1754. It is also worth visiting the catacombs, where the mortal remains of 15 early Habsburgs rest in peace, as well as the organs of another 56 members of the dynasty preserved in urns here while their bodies are buried in the Imperial Vault. If you manage to climb up the 343 narrow steps to the Tower Keeper's Room in the South Tower, you will be rewarded with a fairytale view over the city. *Mon–Sat 9-11.30am, 1.30-4.30pm, Sun 1.30-4.30pm | audio-guided tours 6 euros | guided evening tours incl. roof tour: look for dates online, booking required; catacombs (only with a guide) Mon-Sat 10-11.30am, 1.30-4.30pm, Sun afternoons approx. every half hour | admission 6 euros; South Tower daily 9am-5.15pm | admission 5.50 euros; lift to the Pummerin in the North Tower daily 9am-8pm | admission 6 euros; all-inclusive ticket with audio guide 20 euros | Stephansplatz 3 | stephanskirche.at | U1, U3 Stephansplatz | ⏱ 2 ½ hrs | ⬚ c6-7*

🚻 ÖFFENTLICHE BEDÜRFNIS-ANSTALT AM GRABEN 🐷

We all need to use the facilities – especially after a busy day's sightseeing – and usually we want to get it all over with as quickly as possible, and without looking at anything too closely. However, if you shut your eyes in the public toilet on Graben, then you'll miss out on Vienna's most beautiful restroom and an officially listed building, with marble, brass, gilded lettering, and a small sink and mirror in every cubicle. This Art Nouveau toilet, the first subterranean public lavatory in Vienna, was built in the Old Town in 1905. You can find the entrances to the left and right of the Josefsbrunnen fountain, just a few metres away from the plague column. *Graben, corner of Habsburgergasse | bus 1A, 2A, U1, U3 Stephansplatz | ⬚ b6*

🎭 TIME TRAVEL VIENNA 🎪 👥

Do you need a quick introduction to Vienna? The 50-minute multisensory experience on offer here will whisk you through the most important events in over 2,000 years of history – from waltzes and Habsburgs to *Sachertorte*, Ottoman wars and plenty of other proud and not-so-proud moments in Vienna's past. The attraction features a 5D cinema and a puppet show, and is set in the basement of the Salvatorian Monastery. It's perfect for those who know nothing about Vienna, although more knowledgeable visitors will find it less appealing. *Daily 10am-8pm | admission 19.90 euros (online 16.90 euros), children (5-14) 15.90 euros (online 13.90 euros) | Habsburgergasse 10a | timetravel-vienna.at | bus 2A Habsburgergasse | U1, U3 Stephansplatz | U3 Herrengasse n| ☉ 1 hr | ▭ b6*

🟥 MUSEUM DER ILLUSIONEN 👥

The Museum of Illusions has three exhibition rooms, where your fellow human beings shrink and grow or stick to the ceiling. This small museum challenges children with wooden toys and puzzles. Bring your camera! *Mon-Fri 10am-6pm, Sat/Sun 10am-7pm | admission 14 euros, children (5-18) 10 euros | Wallnerstrasse 4 | museumderillusionen.at | U 3 Herrengasse | ☉ 1 hr | ▭ b6*

🟥 PALAIS FERSTEL

This showpiece of Ringstrasse architecture was erected for the National Bank by Heinrich von Ferstel between 1865 and 1870. It was also the home of the Stock Exchange until 1877. On its ground floor, *Café Central*, on the corner of Herrengasse and Strauchgasse, was famous as a meeting place for men of letters at around the turn of the 20th century. After decades of decay, the gigantic building complex, with entrances on three sides, and its shopping arcades, was finally restored in the 1980s. *Freyung 2/Herrengasse | bus 1A, 2A, U3 Herrengasse | ▭ b6*

🟥 FREYUNG

In the Middle Ages, this large, triangular open space in the north-west of the Old Town served as a marketplace, a stage for clowns and an execution site.

The Babenberg Duke Heinrich II Jasomirgott founded the *Schottenstift* Benedictine abbey on the north side in 1155. Many magnificent palaces were built around the Freyung, including the Baroque *Palais Daun-Kinsky* (No. 4) by Lukas von Hildebrandt, the *Palais Harrach* (No. 3) and the Venetian-style *Palais Ferstel* (No. 2), along with the famous *Café Central*. You should also take a closer look at the so-called *Schubladenhaus* (Chest-of-Drawers House) to the right of the Schottenkirche. *Bus 1A, 2A, U3 Herrengasse | ▭ b6*

🟥 BANK AUSTRIA KUNSTFORUM

A changing programme of high-quality exhibitions of 19th- and 20th-century painting can be found here, displayed in galleries designed by star architect Gustav Peichl. *Sat-Thu 10am-7pm, Fri 10am-9pm | admission 12 euros, Happy Hour (2 people for the price of 1) Mon-Thu 6-7pm| Freyung 8 | kunstforumwien.at | tram D, 1, 37, 38, 40-44, 71, U2 Schottentor | bus 1A, 2A, U3 Herrengasse | ▭ b6*

🟥 AM HOF

The "Hof" – the court of the Dukes of Babenberg – was already standing in the original centre of the city in the 12th century. A good 100 years later, the ruler's seat moved to the Hofburg, but the square's feudal flair has been preserved to this day. The *Mariensäule* (Column of the Virgin Mary) stands in the centre of the square. It is surrounded by a series of impressive façades: the *Church of the Nine Choirs* of Angels and *Palais Collalto*, where the six-year-old Mozart gave his first concert in Vienna, to the left; opposite, the *Marklein House*, designed by JL von Hildebrandt and the "Citizens' Armoury" with the 🐷 *Fire Brigade Museum (Tue 2–5pm, Sun 9am–noon | admission free | Am Hof 7). Bus 1A, 2A | 🕮 b6*

40 MARIA AM GESTADE

The main attraction of this slender Gothic church (built 1343–1414), which once stood directly on the steep bank of an arm of the Danube, is the seven-sided, helmet-shaped filigree spire on top of its steeple. The bend in the axis between the nave and choir, as a result of the terrain, is an architecturally interesting element. The relics of St Clemens Maria Hofbauer, the patron saint of Vienna, are kept in a shrine in front of the altar in a side chapel. *Salvatorgasse 12/Passauer Platz | bus 1A, 3A | 🕮 b6*

41 DOKUMENTATIONSARCHIV DES ÖSTERREICHISCHEN WIDERSTANDS

How did the Nazi dictatorship in Austria come about? Who was persecuted and who dared to resist? And what happened at the end of World War II? These and many other questions are answered by the somewhat hidden Documentation Centre of Austrian Resistance, in a permanent exhibition. Interesting display boards explain the *Anschluss* (the annexation of Austria) and the resistance of the Carinthian Slovenes, as well as postwar right-wing extremism. Apart from photographs and illustrated texts, you can find original documents from the Nazi era. *Mon–Wed, Fri 9am–5pm, Thu 9am–7pm | admission free |*

Little Venice in Freyung: a café in the Palais Ferstel

A popular selfie spot in the Stadtpark: Johann Strauss Jr plays a waltz

Wipplingerstrasse 6–8 | doew.at, virtual exhibition at ausstellung.de.doew | U1, U3 Stephansplatz | ⏱ 30 mins | 🗺 c6

42 HOHER MARKT

Foundations and sections of the wall of the Vindobona Roman legions' camp were discovered underneath the pavement of the oldest square in Vienna, which was also the site of the city's dungeons, pillory and court building in the Middle Ages. The remains of Roman officers' houses can be seen in a subterranean showroom, *Römermuseum (Tue–Sun 9am–6pm | admission 7 euros)*. Another attraction, the *Ankeruhr*, can be found in the north-east corner of the square: in 1911, the Art Nouveau artist Franz von Matsch joined the buildings at Nos. 10 and 11 with a bridge-like construction and an artistic clock. Twelve figures from the history of Vienna appear over 12 hours and there is a parade of the entire group, complete with music, every day at noon. *Bus 1A, 3A, U1, U3 Stephansplatz | U1, U4 Schwedenplatz | 🗺 c6*

43 STADTTEMPEL

Nothing could be less impressive at first sight, as it's hard to imagine that Vienna's main synagogue is concealed behind the façade of an apartment building at No. 4 Seitenstettengasse. The reason why it's impossible to recognise the Stadttempel as a house of prayer from the outside is because at the time of its construction in 1826, non-Catholic places of worship were not allowed to be visible from the street. However, it's thanks to the building's unassuming façade that this was the only one of Vienna's 94 synagogues to survive the *Kristallnacht* pogrom in 1938.

The entrance hall contains a memorial to the 65,000 Austrian Jews who were murdered during the war, with their names engraved on movable slate tablets. Make sure you bring some photo ID with you and factor in plenty of time for the security checks. Visits only possible as part of a guided tour. Tickets available online. *Mon–Fri 10–11am | Seitenstettengasse 4 | jewishinfopoint.at | U4 Schwedenplatz | ⏱ 1 hr | ⑾ c6*

44 RUPRECHTSKIRCHE

The oldest preserved church in Vienna stands right in the "Bermuda Triangle" entertainment area. It is said that tiny St Rupert's foundations have been standing since 740 CE. Its nave is Romanesque from the 12th century. *Ruprechtsplatz 1 | bus 2A, U1, U4 Schwedenplatz | ⑾ c6*

45 ÖSTERREICHISCHE POSTSPARKASSE ☞

The great innovator Otto Wagner, who always championed the unity of functionality and beauty, and whose buildings shaped Vienna's cityscape, created one of the pioneering feats of modern architecture – and his own masterpiece – with the Postal Savings Bank. The exterior, faced with sheets of marble and granite, and crowned with two aluminium guardian angels, and the glass-roofed main hall, where the interior decoration was planned to perfection, are worth seeing. *Main hall: Mon–Fri 1–6pm | admission free | Georg-Coch-Platz 2 | tram 2 Julius-Raab-Platz | ⏱ 1 hr | ⑾ d6*

46 MAK – MUSEUM FÜR ANGEWANDTE KUNST

European arts and crafts from the Middle Ages to the present day: glass, ceramics, furniture, porcelain, textiles, as well as Eastern Asian artefacts: the collection in the Museum of Applied Arts is not only extensive but also presented very effectively. Highlights include objects from the Wiener Werkstätte art workshop and oriental carpets. In addition, there are regular, fascinating exhibitions of modern art. The museum building, designed by the architect Heinrich von Ferstel, with a richly decorated red-brick façade in the style of the Italian Renaissance, is also worth special attention. ☞ No plans for Tuesday evening yet? From 6–9pm, admission to the MAK is only 7 euros. *Tue 10am–9pm, Wed–Sun 10am–6pm | admission 15 euros | Stubenring 5 | mak.at | tram 2, bus 3A, 74A, U3 Stubentor | ⏱ 1 hr | ⑾ d6-7*

INSIDER TIP
Discounted art

47 STADTPARK

This green island of tranquillity was opened in 1862 and was the first park to be established by the city administration. Its serpentine paths are lined with monuments. The most famous shows Johann Strauss Jr getting his orchestra ready to perform a waltz. The beautiful stairways and pavilions next to the Stadtpark underground station – designed by the Art Nouveau architect Friedrich Ohmann – have been painstakingly renovated. *Parkring | U4 Stadtpark | tram 2, U3 Stubentor | ⊞ d7*

Everything at MQ Point carries the MQ (Museumsquartier) logo

48 JESUITENKIRCHE

The most fascinating aspect of the Jesuit Church is its illusionist ceiling painting that creates the impression of a dome in the middle of the nave. The church (also known as the University Church) was built in the 17th century, before being redecorated in the High Baroque style by Andrea Pozzo in the early 18th century. Its two-towered façade lines one of the most charming squares in the city centre. *Dr-Ignaz-Seipel-Platz | tram 2, bus 2A, U3 Stubentor | ⊞ d6*

49 MOZARTHAUS

The master lived in this late Rococo house – the only one of Mozart's many residences in Vienna to have been preserved – between 1784 and 1787, and the opera *The Marriage of Figaro* was one of the major works composed here. The building has been entirely renovated and now houses a comprehensive overview of Wolfgang Amadeus Mozart's Viennese years. *Tue–Sun 10am–6pm, July/Aug 10am–7pm | admission 12 euros | Domgasse 5 | mozarthausvienna.at | bus 1A, U1, U3 Stephansplatz | ⊞ c6*

NEUBAU, JOSEFSTADT & ALSERGRUND

With the opening of the Museumsquartier – the MQ – at the beginning of the millennium, Neubau, in the 7th District, developed into a hotspot for art freaks and trend scouts.

Even before that, the once-depressing, congested *Gürtel* at its western border had metamorphosed into a chic cultural and gastronomic area. Now, fashionable bars and restaurants, boutiques, and quirky arts and crafts shops are shooting up like mushrooms in the streets in between. The charming *Biedermeier Spittelberg* district is a model of idyllic urban life. The neighbouring *Josefstadt* district has long enjoyed a reputation as a

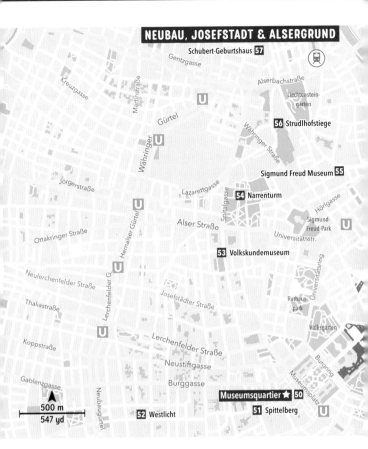

NEUBAU, JOSEFSTADT & ALSERGRUND

Schubert-Geburtshaus **57**

56 Strudlhofstiege

Sigmund Freud Museum **55**

54 Narrenturm

Sigmund-Freud-Park

53 Volkskundemuseum

Rathaus-park

Volksgarten

Museumsquartier ★ **50**

52 Westlicht   **51** Spittelberg

500 m
547 yd

culture zone – albeit a rather bourgeois one – mainly due to the theatre of the same name. Most of the architecture here in the 8th District, and in the 9th to the north in *Alsergrund*, dates from the 19th century. The Old General Hospital is now home not to doctors and their patients, but to professors and their students, as the University of Vienna has moved in with a number of its institutes. There are plenty of cheap and tasty places to eat in the university area.

50 MUSEUMSQUARTIER ★

If you love art and culture, there's no getting around the Museumsquartier – or MQ. In 2001, a unique museum complex was opened on the 60,000-m² site of the former Court Stables after a thorough redevelopment of the area. Together with the Kunsthistorisches Museum and Museum of Natural History on the other side of Museumsplatz and the Hofburg, one of the largest artistic districts in the world was created. More than 20 museums, initiatives and projects have been established here and make the Museumsquartier both an artistic laboratory and place for experimentation and theoretical reflection, and a location where art is produced and presented. Gigantic lounges in the inner courtyard invite visitors to muse, chat and relax.

INSIDER TIP
Take-away art The *Buchhandlung Walther König* bookshop in the MQ's central corridor has a superb selection of current art catalogues and books.

The *Leopold Museum (Wed–Mon 10am–6pm, daily in July/Aug | admission 15 euros | leopoldmuseum.org)* – with the world's largest collection of works by Egon Schiele as well as masterpieces by Gustav Klimt, Oskar Kokoschka, Alfred Kubin and many others – is one of the most important institutions in the MQ. Another is the ☎ *Museum Moderner Kunst (Museum of Modern Art, Tue–Sun 10am–6pm | admission 14 euros, children under 18 free | mumok.at)* with collections of classic modern art, the Austrian avant-garde of the post-war years, and important contemporary movements such as Informel, Photorealism, and Object and Action Art. Children from four years of age can tour the museum on a *"KinderkunstTransporter"* which also contains painting equipment.

The same area also houses the headquarters of the *Kunsthalle (Tue/Wed, Fri–Sun 11am–7pm, Thu 11am–9pm | admission 8 euros | kunsthallewien.at)*, the *Architekturzentrum Wien (azw.at)*, the *Tanzquartier Wien*

An environmentally friendly lunch in the Spittelberg, in Siebensterngasse *(tqw.at)*, two halls for events and experimental spaces in the fields of film, new media and art theory called Quartier 21, as well as the 🎭 *Jungle Theatre (dschungelwien.at)* and the 🎭 *Zoom Kindermuseum (Tue–Fri 9.15am–1.15pm, Sat/Sun 9.15am–5pm | admission from 5 euros | kindermuseum.at)*. Here you will find the *Ocean*, an interactive dance performance (for babies to six-year-olds), a studio for child artists (aged 3–12) and a multimedia laboratory for experimenting with animated cartoons, sound and 3D (for children 8–14).

With its 10 entrances and exits, and numerous cafés and restaurants, the MQ is an attractive stop between the city centre and the neighbouring districts, and it pulsates with life until late at night. *Museumsplatz 1 | tel. 01 5 23 58 81 | mqw.at | tram 49, bus 48A, U2, U3 Volkstheater or Museumsquartier |* ⏱ *from 2 hrs |* 🗺 *a8*

🔢 SPITTELBERG

In the Middle Ages, cows used to graze here; later, wine was cultivated on the hill. Today, the narrow, pedestrianised lanes behind the Museumsquartier are lined with small Biedermeier houses with cosy shops, restaurants and cafés. With its art market, Spittelberg is especially charming at Christmastime. *Tram 49, bus 48A, U2, U3 Volkstheater |* 🗺 *J9*

🔢 WESTLICHT

From war photography and images from space to historical portraits of famous figures such as Che Guevara, this museum of photography and photographic art features pictures that changed and are changing the world, displayed in a programme of six to eight exhibitions per year that includes the World Press Photo competition. There is also a large collection of antique cameras. Particularly fascinating is a miniature panorama camera that the German Army fitted to pigeons in World War I. *Tue, Wed, Fri 2–7pm, Thu 2–9pm, Sat/Sun 11am–7pm | admission 9 euros | Westbahnstr. 40 | westlicht.com | tram 5, 49, U6 Burggasse-Stadthalle | U3 Zieglergasser |* ⏱ *45 mins |* 🗺 *H9*

INSIDER TIP
World War I photo drone

🔢 VOLKSKUNDEMUSEUM 🎐

The *Gartenpalais Schönborn* (Garden Palace) is home to Vienna's folklore museum, with a collection of more than 100,000 everyday objects: on display are textiles, ceramics and furniture, plus a photographic collection of tens of thousands of images. A permanent exhibition features the European refugee crisis of 2015: "The Shores of Austria" was curated by asylum seekers. There are also panel discussions, readings and book launches, which are announced on the website. *Tue/Wed, Fri–Sun 10am–5pm, Thu 10am–8pm | admission 8 euros | Laudongasse 15–19 | volkskundemuseum.at | bus 13A, tram 5, 33 Laudongasse | tram 43, 44 Lange Gasse |* ⏱ *1–2 hrs |* 🗺 *H7*

🔢 NARRENTURM

Take a deep breath and try not to feel queasy: the pathological anatomy

After climbing the Strudlhofstiege steps, you deserve an apple strudel!

museum in the Narrenturm is packed with organs and deformed foetuses floating in glass jars. The collection boasts 45,000 specimens, making it the largest of its kind. The building on the Altes AKH university campus is also nicknamed the Guglhupf, due to its resemblance to the cake of the same name, and was built by Emperor Joseph II as the first institution in Europe to be dedicated exclusively to the treatment of psychiatric conditions.

INSIDER TIP
A beer in the hospital

Apart from indulging your medical interests, the inner university courtyards of the Altes AKH are ideal for relaxing in summer, and you can get a drink in the Stiegl-Ambulanz restaurant. *Altes AKH campus daily,*

Narrenturm Wed 10am–6pm, Thu/Fri 10am–3pm, Sat noon–6pm | admission 8 euros (taking photographs not permitted!), guided tour 4 euros | Spitalgasse 2 | nhm-wien.ac.at | tram 5, 33, 43, 44 Lange Gasse | U2 Schottentor | ⊞ H7

55 SIGMUND FREUD MUSEUM

Manuscripts and other memorabilia are displayed in the rooms where the father of psychoanalysis had his offices for almost half a century – until he was forced to leave Austria in 1938. However, the famous couch for Freud's patients is not among the exhibits. *Wed–Mon 10am–6pm | admission 14 euros | Berggasse 19 | freud-museum. at | tram D, 37, 38, 40–42, bus 40A Berggasse | ⊙ 45 mins | ⊞ J6*

56 STRUDLHOFSTIEGE ⚑

This elegant flight of steps climbs the slope between Währinger Strasse and Palais Liechtenstein. It achieved literary fame in a novel by Heimito von Doderer. Doderer describes the exquisite construction decorated with wrought-iron Art Nouveau lanterns created in 1910 to plans drawn up by Johann Theodor Jäger as "the terrace-like stage of the drama of life". *Strudlhofgasse 8 | near Liechtensteinstr. | tram D, bus 40A Bauernfeldplatz | ⌑ J6*

57 SCHUBERT-GEBURTSHAUS

The prince of song, Franz Schubert, first saw the light of day in this typical old Viennese suburban house on 31 January 1797. Besides biographical documents and portraits, Schubert's famous glasses are on display. A room dedicated to the writer Adalbert Stifter is attached to the museum. *Tue–Sun 10am–1pm, 2–6pm | admission 5 euros | Nussdorfer Str. 54 | wien musum.at | tram 37, 38 Canisiusgasse | ⏲ 30 mins | ⌑ H–J5*

MARIAHILF, MARGARETEN & WIEDEN

This is one of the trendiest areas of Vienna: on both sides of the Wien River, near the flea market and Naschmarkt.

The narrow – and often quite steep – streets in *Mariahilf*, in the 6th District, are lined with artists' cafés, trendy bars and independent shops. The same applies to the two neighbouring districts to the south, especially the area between Pilgram and Kettenbrückengasse, as well as the *Freihausviertel* to the east. A stroll through the *Naschmarkt*, a food market known as "the belly of Vienna", is something like a pilgrimage for the senses. Mainstream shoppers, meanwhile, will feel that they are in heaven on *Mariahilfer Strasse*, the street with the greatest variety of shops in Vienna.

MARIAHILF, MARGARETEN & WIEDEN

Map showing: Stollgasse, Lindengasse, 59 Hofmobiliendepot Möbel-Museum Wien, Wienzeile, Operngasse, Karlskirche 64, 60 Haus des Meeres, 61 Majolikahaus, 63 Freihausviertel, Esterházygasse, Linke, Rechte, 58 Mariahilfer Strasse, 62 Dritte-Mann-Museum, Bürgerspitalgasse, Stumpergasse, Gumpendorfer Str., Hofmühlgasse, Schönbrunner Straße, Margaretenstraße, Gußhausstr., Moллardgasse, Pilgramgasse, Mittersteig, Wiedner Hauptstraße, Favoritenstraße, Schönbrunner Str., Gartengasse

▲
500 m
547 yd

This is an area without many sight-seeing highlights. However, the Art Nouveau architect Otto Wagner designed two beautiful houses on the Linke Wienzeile, the *Theater an der Wien*, which is steeped in history, is just down the street and *Karlsplatz* is dominated by the Baroque church of the same name.

58 MARIAHILFER STRASSE

No other street in Vienna has been the subject of so much controversy: in 2014, the Mahü (as it is known by residents) was pedestrianised, in the face of staunch opposition. Although local traders foresaw the death of the retail trade here, the street is flourishing – with café after café appearing among its many shops. Children will find plenty of places to play in the pedestrian zone, giving their parents a chance to relax after a busy day's shopping. *Tram 6, 9, 18, 52, 60, bus 2A, 13A, 14A Zieglergasse & Neubaugasse | U3, U6 Westbahnhof | U2, U3 Volkstheater | U2 Museumsquartier | ▥ G–J 9–10*

59 HOFMOBILIENDEPOT MÖBEL-MUSEUM WIEN

Empress Sisi kept her dressing tables here, while her beloved Franzl stored the wardrobes from his hunting lodge. The Imperial Furniture Collection was originally the Habsburgs' furniture warehouse, and over the last few centuries it has grown into one of the biggest collections of household effects in the world. Vienna's furniture museum tells the story of changing tastes in interior decor with the help of 165,000 different objects, covering styles from the Biedermeier period to historicism, the Wiener Moderne and contemporary design. *Tue–Sun 10am–5pm | admission 11.50 euros | Andreasgasse 7/Mariahilfer Str. 88 | moebelmuseum.at | U3 Zieglergasse | ⊙ from 2 hrs | ▥ H10*

60 HAUS DES MEERES ☂ 👪

The hammerhead sharks may be small compared to their wild relatives, but they are nonetheless the biggest attraction in Vienna's aquarium. This former Nazi flak tower once served as a refuge for local people, and is now home to the aquatic inhabitants of lakes and oceans. You'll even find snakes and monkeys here, too. The view from the rooftop café over Vienna's streets is sensational. *Daily 9am–8pm | admission 21.90 euros, children (3–5) 6.50 euros, (6–15) 9.80 euros | Fritz-Grünbaum-Platz 1 | haus-des-meeres.at | U3 Neubaugasse | bus 13A, 14A Haus des Meeres | ⊙ from 2 hrs | ▥ J10*

61 MAJOLIKAHAUS

The block of flats – created by famous Austrian architect Otto Wagner, with a façade of weatherproof ceramic tiles decorated with colorful images of interwined plants – is a feast for the eyes for all Art Nouveau fans. The house on the corner to the right, with its filigree golden decoration, was also designed by Wagner. The medallions of women's heads were created by Kolo Moser, one of the co-founders of the Secession art movement and Wiener Werkstätte. *Linke Wienzeile 38/40 | U4 Kettenbrückengasse | ▥ J10*

Karlskirche: a lift takes you to the platform with a view of the cupola fresco

🔢 DRITTE-MANN-MUSEUM 🛗

Near Karlsplatz you can embark on a journey into Vienna's underworld by taking a tour *(drittemanntour.at)* that follows in the footsteps of Orson Welles. Here, below the city's streets in Vienna's sewer system, is where scenes from *The Third Man* were filmed in 1948. Fans of the movie who prefer to stay above ground can visit the museum instead, which contains over 2,300 original pieces of memorabilia relating to the cinema classic, as well as background information about post-war Vienna. You haven't watched *The Third Man*? The Burgkino cinema at the Opernring shows the black-and-white thriller in English every Tuesday and Sunday. *Museum Sat 2–6pm, with guided tours of the sewer system | admission*

INSIDER TIP
Murderer, murderer!

museum 9.50 euros | Pressgasse 25 | 3mpc.net | bus 59A Pressgasse | U4 Kettenbrückengasse | ⏱ 1 hr | 🗺 K10

🔢 FREIHAUSVIERTEL

An extremely trendy area has established itself around Schleifmühlgasse – with galleries and a number of chic cafés and restaurants, and shops that are often open until late in the evening. *U4 Kettenbrückengasse | U1 Taubstummengasse | 🗺 K10*

🔢 KARLSKIRCHE 🚩

After the plague had wiped out more than 8,000 Viennese in 1713, Emperor Karl VI vowed to build a church dedicated to the saint who had once helped those suffering from the Black Death in Milan, St Charles Borromeo, if the horror were to end quickly. The votive building on Karlsplatz by Johann Bernhard Fischer von Erlach was consecrated in 1737 and is considered one of the greatest masterpieces of European Baroque architecture. A glazed lift leads up to a 32m-high platform from where you can see the monumental fresco in the

LEOPOLD-STADT & LANDSTRASSE

A popular Viennese song celebrates spring, "when the flowers bloom again in the Prater", and that really is the season when young and old swarm outside to walk or play sport on the main road through the area, the Hauptallee, and in the surrounding woods.

The Giant Ferris Wheel is another major attraction in the *Leopoldstadt*, with the Volksprater (People's Prater) or Wurstelprater at its feet. The labyrinth of streets between Nestroyplatz and Karmelitermarkt – until the onslaught of Nazi terror, the traditional home of Viennese Jews – has also become increasingly fashionable in recent years.

The 3rd District, known as Landstrasse, lies on the other side of the Danube Canal. It shows its most impressive side in and around Belvedere. The adjacent residential and embassy area is also elegant, while things become more down-to-earth near the Rochusmarkt and along Landstrasser Hauptstrasse. There are many government offices in the area, as well as the Music University, the Konzerthaus and Akademietheater.

The Giant Ferris Wheel (*Riesenrad*) in the Prater: 10 minutes of happiness

cupola up close. In the summer, concerts, festivals and open-air films take place on the square in front of the church. *Mon–Fri 7.30am–7pm, Sat 8.30am–7pm, Sun 9am–7pm | admission incl. lift 8 euros | Karlsplatz | karlskirche.info | tram D, 71, U1, U2, U4 Karlsplatz/Oper | ⌐ c8*

65 PRATER ★ ⚑

The Viennese made this almost 15km-long landscaped area of woods and meadows with backwaters

LEOPOLDSTADT & LANDSTRASSE

Ausstellungsstraße

500m
547 yd

Messe Wien

65 Prater ★

Praterstraße

Untere Donaustraße

66 Kunst Haus Wien

Weißgerberlände

Stubenring

Vordere Zollamtsstr.

Fälschermuseum 68

67 Hundertwasserhaus

Park Prater

Jesuitenwiese

Kundmanng.

Landstraßer

Wassergasse

Schüttelstraße

Erdberger Lände

Stadionallee

Ungargasse

69 Russisch-orthodoxe Kathedrale

Hauptstraße

Schlachthausgasse

Erdbergstraße

Rennweg

70 Belvedere ★

Belvedere 21 71

72 Heeresgeschichtliches Museum ★

running through it their own as a recreation area after Emperor Joseph II
opened up the imperial hunting
grounds to all in 1766. Today, the
Prater is still one of the city's main
"green lungs", with cycle paths and
footpaths, tennis courts, a golf course,
a trotting and racing track, and cycling
and football stadiums.

A hotchpotch of amusement parks
and inns, the so-called *Volksprater* or
Wurstelprater, was established in the
western section close to the city in
the early 19th century. On the edge,
and somewhat hid-
den, is a small
ball-shaped house
with a bizarre history:
in 1976, the artist Edwin Lipburger
declared his studio an autonomous
republic named "Kugelmugel".

INSIDER TIP
Stop! State border!

He had erected the building without planning permission and resisted
the authorities for several years. In the
end, he was sent to prison for 10
weeks and the Kugelmugel art project
was subsequently moved into the
Prater.

You can still feel something of the nostalgic charm of the Wurstelprater amusement park in the old-fashioned ghost trains, hall of mirrors, shooting galleries and beer gardens, although glittery hi-tech catapult rides have started to take over. The 10-minute ride on the Giant Ferris Wheel, the ⚑ *Riesenrad (daily Nov–Feb 10am–7.45pm, March–April, Oct & Christmastime 10am–9.45pm, end April–early Sept 9am–11.45pm, Sept 9am–10.45pm | 13.50 euros | wiener riesenrad.com | N6)*, is a must for all visitors to Vienna. This 67m-high city landmark, built in iron, was erected in 1897 and became world-famous when it was used as one of the settings in Carol Reed's post-war thriller *The Third Man*. The 🐵 *Liliputbahn*, a 4km-long miniature narrow-gauge railway, has its station not far away. Next door, the *Planetarium (tel. 01 8 91 74 15 00 00)* will take you on an excursion to the starry skies. At the northern edge of the Prater is the extensive car-free campus of the *Wirtschaftsuniversität (WU) Wien* (University of Economics and Business), with its exciting architecture. At its heart is the futuristic *Library & Learning Center*, designed by star architect Zaha Hadid. *Wurstelprater | prater.at | tram O, 1, 5, S-Bahn 1, 3, 7, 15, U1, U2 Praterstern | N–S 6–11*

🏛 KUNST HAUS WIEN

This multicoloured museum has a permanent display of Friedensreich Hundertwasser's work, as well as temporary exhibitions of works by other well-known artists. *Daily 10am–6pm | admission 12 euros | Untere Weissgerberstr. 13 | kunsthaus wien.com | tram 1, O Radetzkyplatz | ⏱ 1–2 hrs | N7*

My home is my castle: Prince Eugene received his guests in Belvedere Palace

67 HUNDERTWASSERHAUS

This block of council flats is a creation of the artist Friedensreich Hundertwasser (1928–2000) (initially in cooperation with the architect Joseph Krawina), which ignores all the rules of symmetry and right angles. Bushes and trees grow on the roofs and balconies, many of the walls and floors are curved and the façades are painted in all the colours of the rainbow. Out of consideration for the people living there, it is usually only possible to see the outside of the building *(Kegelgasse 34–38/ Löwengasse | tram 1 Hetzgasse)*. However, Hundertwasser's *Toilet of Modern Art* in the *Kalke Village shopping arcade (Kegelgasse 37–39)* is open for public use. The artist's fans should also not miss out on visiting the Spittelau waste incineration plant, decorated by the master, next to the U4 or U6 Spittelau U-Bahn station. ⌐ N8

INSIDER TIP
Artistic waste treatment

68 FÄLSCHERMUSEUM

The Museum of Art Fakes is the only one of its kind in Europe. It offers fascinating background information on the criminal sides of painting and the art business. It also shows 60 fakes and copies of works by great masters. Very entertaining! *Tue-Fri 10am–4pm, Sat/Sun 10am–5pm | admission 6.50 euros | Löwengasse 28 | faelschermuseum.com | tram 1 Hetzgasse | ⏱ 1 hr | ⌐ N8*

69 RUSSISCH-ORTHODOXE KATHEDRALE

An impressive building that can be seen from afar: the Russian Orthodox St Nicholas Cathedral, with its five golden domes and colourful roof tiles, dates from 1899. The interior is adorned with sky-blue and gold frescoes and icons showing important scenes from the life of St Nicholas. *Sun-Fri 10am–2pm, Sat 10am–1pm | Jaurèsgasse 2 | nikolsobor.org | S-Bahn Rennweg | tram O Ungargasse/ Neulinggasse | U4 Stadtpark | ⌐ M9*

70 BELVEDERE ★ ⚑

Prince Eugene of Savoy's former summer palace is a must for every visitor to Vienna. The spacious complex, with its two palaces, is not only considered Johann Lukas von Hildebrandt's masterpiece but also one of the world's most magnificent Baroque buildings.

The general and conqueror of the Turks from Savoy had the *Obere Belvedere (Upper Belvedere, 1721–23)* built on a slightly elevated site, with all of Vienna at its feet, purely for representational purposes. The long, superbly proportioned building now houses a gallery for Austrian art in its lavish interior. The main focus is on local classics from the Biedermeier (Ferdinand Georg Waldmüller, Rudolf von Alt), late-Romantic and late 19th-century periods (Leopold Kupelwieser, Hans Makart), and Art Nouveau, Expressionism and post-war art (Egon Schiele, Oskar Kokoschka). In addition, major works of international art form part of the collection, including paintings by

Caspar David Friedrich, Claude Monet, Vincent van Gogh, Emil Nolde and Edvard Munch. However, the real crowd-puller is Gustav Klimt and especially his painting *The Kiss*, one of the most important Art Nouveau works. There is also a Baroque collection and medieval masterpieces.

Prince Eugene actually lived in the *Untere Belvedere* (Lower Belvedere, 1714–16), an only minimally less impressive building, which also has a marble hall ornately decorated with frescos and stucco, a hall of mirrors and a state gallery. Temporary exhibitions of modern or contemporary art are presented in the adjacent *Orangerie* and other artworks from the Middle Ages are in the nearby state stables.

The two palaces are linked by a garden more than 500m long that has been returned to its original Baroque style. *Upper Belvedere daily 10am–6pm, Lower Belvedere Sat–Thu 10am–6pm, Fri 10am–9pm, Garden daily 6.30am–5.30pm, until 9pm in summer | admission Upper Belvedere 16.90 euros, Lower Belvedere 14.90 euros, combined ticket 25 euros | belvedere.at | Upper Belvedere: Prinz-Eugen-Str. 27 | Lower Belvedere: Rennweg 6a | Upper Belvedere: tram D, 18 Schloss Belvedere | Lower Belvedere: tram 71 Unteres Belvedere | ⏱ from 2 hrs | ⅏ M10*

⚀ BELVEDERE 21

This architecturally stunning pavilion from the late 1950s is located within view of Vienna's new central train station, and offers exciting encounters with Austrian art from 1945 to the present day in an international context. *Tue–Sun 11am–6pm | admission 8.90 euros | Arsenalstr. 1 | Schweizergarten | belvedere.at | tram D, 18, 0 Quartier Belvedere | ⏱ 1 hr | ⅏ M11*

⚁ HEERESGESCHICHTLICHES MUSEUM ★

A real gem for anyone with an interest in military history. Inside this elaborate complex of Moorish and neo-Gothic architecture you can find an exhibition on the eventful history of the Habsburg army and navy, which documents the Thirty Years' War, the Ottoman wars, World War I and the Republican era in superb detail. Fascinating! *Daily 9am–5pm | admission 7 euros | Arsenal 1 | hgm.at | tram D, 18, 0 Quartier Belvedere | ⏱ 1 hr | ⅏ N11–12*

OTHER SIGHTS

⚂ LAINZER TIERGARTEN 🐗

The Vienna Woods, extending over 1,250km², surround the metropolis in a semi-circle on the west, and are the subject of songs, poems and waltz melodies. A 25-km² section of it, the so-called Lainzer Tiergarten animal park, lets you encounter wild animals, from wild boars to carp, for free. The 80km of waymarked paths and several snack bars invite visitors to go on lengthy hikes *(May–early Jan daily*

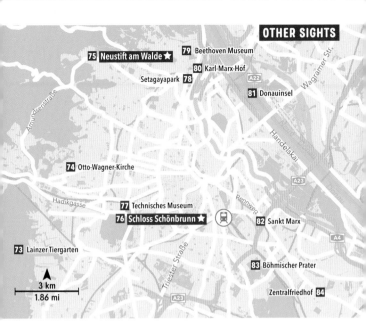

8am–nightfall). You have a lovely view of the wooded surroundings from the top of the *Hubertuswarte*. The *Hermesvilla (March–end Oct Tue–Sun 10am–6pm | admission 7 euros | wienmuseum.at | U4 Hietzing, then tram 60, 62 from Hermesstrasse stop | bus 60B)*, a hunting lodge built in 1882–86, which is now used for interesting exhibitions as a branch of the Historisches Museum, is the most noteworthy attraction in the wildlife preserve. | *Hietzing* | 🗺 b2

74 OTTO-WAGNER-KIRCHE

This was the last lucrative commission undertaken by the architect Otto Wagner. Archduke Franz Ferdinand's conservative tastes meant he was never the biggest fan of Art Nouveau, but this 1907 church, built out of white Carrara marble and topped with golden angels and a Byzantine gold dome, was the last straw. The building even features a toilet, a medical room and emergency exits. Nowadays, the church – officially known as the Kirche am Steinhof or the Church of St Leopold, and located in the middle of a psychiatric institute – is justly recognised as one of the most beautiful buildings of its time. The gorgeous surroundings of the grounds of the nearby Steinhof hospital are also the perfect place to take a stroll. *Sat 2–5pm, Sun 11am–5pm | admission 5 euros | guided tours tel. 01 50 58 74 78 51 80 | Baumgartner Höhe 1 | wienmuseum.at | U4 Unter St. Veit, then bus 47A Klinik Penzing or U3 Ottakring, then bus 46B Feuerwache am Steinhof | Penzing | 🗺 A8*

Heurigen are located amid the vineyards in Neustift am Walde

75 NEUSTIFT AM WALDE ★ ⚑

There are many winemaking districts dotted with *Heurigen* (wine taverns) – from Mauer on the southern city border to Sievering, Heiligenstadt, Nussdorf and Pötzleinsdorf, and Jedlersdorf, Strebersdorf and Stammersdorf on the other side of the Danube. Unfortunately, the odds of being served a glass of dreadful rotgut and charged a fortune for it are relatively high, especially if you visit one of the supposedly "authentic" *Heuriger* taverns in Grinzing to which tourists are carted by the busload. However, in Neustift am Walde this is luckily a rare experience. Here you will still find a host of small family businesses situated picturesquely amid their vineyards, all of which offer something really special. Some of the most beautiful are *Weinhof Zimmermann* (see p. 74), *Fuhrgassl-Huber* (Neustift am Walde 68) and *Zeiler am Hauerweg* (Rathstr. 31). Bus 35A Agnesgasse | U6 Nussdorf | Döbling | ⌑ b1

76 SCHLOSS SCHÖNBRUNN ★ ⚑

Along with St Stephen's Cathedral and the Belvedere, the Habsburgs' summer residence, Schönbrunn Palace – sometimes called Austria's Versailles – is Vienna's main attraction. In spite of all the splendour, the complex does not seem to be at all flashy or pretentious but instead charming and approachable. It has its origins in an old bourgeois manor house that Emperor Maximilian II bought in 1559 and then expanded into a hunting lodge. After it was destroyed by the Turks in 1683, Johann Bernhard Fischer von Erlach planned the building in the basic form we see today, with two side wings, the spacious

Court of Honour facing the street and the flight of steps on the garden side.

Schönbrunn finally became the focal point of the monarchy during the reign of Empress Maria Theresa, who lived here with her husband Franz I Stephan of Lorraine and their 16 children. At her command, the young architect Nicolaus Pacassi remodelled the palace between 1744 and 1749 to adapt it to the late-Baroque taste of the time, adding an additional storey as well as numerous balconies and staircases, creating an impressive carriageway and building the charming Baroque Palace Theatre. The new, elegantly playful, Rococo style found its way into the residential and public rooms.

Some 40 of the most beautiful rooms in the palace, from a total of more than 1,400, can be visited on a guided tour. They include the Great Gallery; the Vieux Laque Room; the Millions Room, with 260 Persian and Indian miniatures embedded into its rosewood panelling; the Napoleon Room, with the gigantic Brussels tapestries; the Chinese Round Room, where Maria Theresa held her secret conferences; and Emperor Franz Joseph's spartan living and working rooms.

The *Wagenburg (Carriage Museum, daily mid-March–Nov 9am–5pm, Dec–mid-March 10am–4pm | admission 12 euros)*, with its unique collection of 60 magnificent state carriages, is housed in a side wing to the west of the Court of Honour and there is a special 👶 children's museum in the main wing. On no account should you miss exploring the beautiful 🐦 *Palace Park*

(daily 6.30am–nightfall | admission free). It includes an enormous *Palm House*, a *maze* and 👶 *Tiergarten*, Vienna's *zoo (daily Oct–Jan 9am–4.30pm, Feb 9am–5pm, March–April 9am–5.30pm, May–Sept 9am–6.30pm | admission 24 euros, children under 6 free, aged 7–18 14 euros | zoovienna.at).* This architectural jewel from the Baroque period, founded in 1752, is considered to be the oldest existing menagerie in the world and even has a special *Desert House*, opposite the Palm House *(Palm House & Desert House daily May–Sept 9am–6pm, Oct–April 9am–5pm | admission 8 euros for each, combined ticket with Zoo 32 euros. Maze daily April–June, July/Aug 9.30am–6pm, Sept/early Oct 9.30am–5pm, Oct 9.30am–4pm | admission 4.50 euros).*

The 🐦 *Gloriette*, which crowns the top of a hill, recalls the victory over Prussia in a battle fought near Kolin in 1757. It is free to visit. The graceful building houses a café with a panoramic roof terrace *(depending on the season, daily 9am–nightfall | admission 4.50 euros).* To let your day at Schönbrunn come to a fitting close, you can listen to a concert in the *Orangerie (tel. 01 8 12 50 04)* or go to an opera performance in the *Marionettentheater (tel. 01 8 17 3247 | marionettentheater.at)* or to the *Palace Theatre*, where operettas and plays are occasionally performed. In the 👶 *Kindermuseum* (children's museum), suitable for children from age seven, palace ghost Poldi tells you all about the everyday life of the Emperor's children's *(daily 10am–5pm*

| admission 8 euros | themed guided tours Sat/Sun and during school holidays daily 10.30am, 1.30pm, 3pm | kaiserkinder.at). The 🎪 Labyrinthikon next to the maze in the park offers various exciting games.

To avoid the queues, you can buy tickets online (imperialtickets.com). There are various combined tickets, from the Schönbrunn Classic Pass (31 euros) to the Family Pass (adults 28 euros, children 23 euros). Show rooms daily Jan–March 9.30am–5pm, April–June, Sept–Dec 9am–5pm, July/Aug 9am–5.30pm | admission Grand Tour (40 rooms) 26 euros, Imperial Tour (22 rooms) 22 euros | schoenbrunn.at | main entrance Schönbrunner, access also through Hietzinger Tor, Hietzinger Hauptstr.; Meidlinger Tor, Grünbergstr.; and Hohenbergstr. | tram 10, 60, bus 10A, 58A, U4 Hietzing & Schönbrunn | ⏱ from 2 hrs | Hietzing | 🗺 D–E12

🟦 TECHNISCHES MUSEUM 🎪

You won't believe your eyes. First there's a Tesla transformer producing lightning bolts that make music. On the floor below it's all aboard for a journey through railway history, with over 150 locomotives and carriages. The Technical Museum shows visitors how technology has changed our lives: from steam locomotives and aeroplanes to racing cars and robots. Young researchers from the age of three can explore a moving landscape of 500m². Parents can create individual puzzle hunts online

INSIDER TIP
For young puzzlers

(10–60 mins) to take with them to the museum. Daily 10am–6pm | admission 14 euros, under 19s free, guided family tours additional 3.50 euros | Mariahilfer Str. 212 | tmw.at | tram 52, 60 Winckelmannstrasse, U4 Schönbrunn | U3 Johnstrasse | ⏱ 1–2 hrs | Penzing | 🗺 E11

🟦 SETAGAYAPARK 🌳

A Japanese feel in Vienna: waterfalls, rock formations and a bamboo gate await you in this Japanese garden to the north of Vienna – a beautiful place to relax! In spring the paths to the tea house are lined with cherry blossom, magnolias and bamboo. After exploring the park, it's worth having a look at the impressive Wienerwald villas in the area. Daily March 7am–6pm, April & Sept 7am–8pm, May–Aug 7am–9pm, Oct 7am–7pm| Hohe Warte 8 | tram 37 Barawitzkagasse | Döbling | 🗺 H–J2

🟦 BEETHOVEN MUSEUM

In Heiligenstadt, Ludwig van Beethoven composed, among other things, the Tempest sonata and developed the concept for what would subsequently be named the Third Symphony (Eroica). It is also where the musician wrote his famous last will in 1802, in which he admitted to his fear of becoming deaf. Tue–Sun 10am–1pm, 2–6pm | admission 7 euros | Probusgasse 6 | wienmuseum.at | tram 37, bus 38A Armbrustergasse | ⏱ 45 mins | Heiligenstadt | 🗺 H1

🟦 KARL-MARX-HOF 🏛

Fortress-like blocks of council flats near the Danube Canal in

Heiligenstadt are impressive witnesses to the heyday of "Red Vienna" in the 1920s. The Karl Marx Hof is a classic example of this revolutionary kind of social housing with which the Social Democratic city council improved the miserable living conditions of the working classes. The complex, planned by Karl Ehn and built in 1927–30, contains 1,600 residential units. The permanent exhibition inside laundry room No. 2 *(Thu 1–6pm, Sun noon–4pm | admission 5 euros | Halteraugasse 7 | dasrotewien-waschsalon.at)*, documenting the progressive municipal politics of Vienna in the 1920s and early 1930s is worth a visit. *Heiligenstädter Str. 82–92/12.-Februar–Platz | tram D, bus 10A, 11A, 39A 12.-Februar-Platz | U4 Heiligenstadt | ○ from 1 hr | Heiligenstadt | ⊞ J1–2*

Getting ready to throw the discus? A sculpture at Karl-Marx-Hof

🔟 DONAUINSEL 🐾 🚩

This artificial island, almost 200m wide and many miles long, between the main river and the excavated channel was created in the 1970s and 1980s as part of extensive flood protection measures. However, it was quickly "occupied" by the Viennese and is now one of the city's most popular recreation areas, where people do sports, have a barbecue or go swimming (in the nude). The *Donauturm (Danube Tower)*, together with the surrounding Donaupark, were created for the International Garden Show in 1964. The tower soars 252m into the sky between the New and Old Danube, a little to the west of the UNO City. There is a wonderful view of Vienna from the revolving restaurant. *Bus 20B Donauturm | Donaustadt | ⊞ L1–S8*

🔟 SANKT MARX 🐾

They say that the Grim Reaper must be Viennese, and there are countless Wienerlied folk songs and proverbs devoted to the topic of death. A long stroll through a cemetery is a balm for the soul in this city – and the most beautiful cemetery of them all is the overgrown graveyard of St Marx, filled with dilapidated gravestones marking the resting place of old Imperial families. Melancholy and romantic. *Daily April–Sept 6.30am–8pm, Oct–March*

6.30am–6.30pm | Leberstr. 6–8 | tram 71 Leberstrasse | Landstrasse | ⌕ O11–12

🎯 BÖHMISCHER PRATER 🎯

Some of the horses are missing the ends of their noses, and the swans sometimes get stuck on the miniature lake. But don't worry – the animals are all made of plastic. Located on the edge of Vienna, this decidedly old-fashioned theme park is the little brother of its more famous namesake. A handful of ageing attractions include a Chair-O-Plane and a Ferris wheel, and there are also a few restaurants, all surrounded by peaceful woodland. That's all there is – but then again, that's all you need, and the setting is gorgeous. The only problem is that it's very difficult to access by public transport. *March–Oct approx. 10am–9pm (weather dependent) | Laaer Wald 216 | böhmischerprater. at | U1 Reumannplatz, then bus 68A Urselbrunnengasse, then 10 mins walk | Favoriten | ⌕ c2*

🏴 ZENTRALFRIEDHOF 🏴

Since its opening in 1874, more than three million people have found their final resting place in the 2.4km² Central Cemetery. The section with the "graves of honour" is especially noteworthy. Many great men and women are buried there, including Franz Schubert, Johann Strauss, Beethoven and Brahms. Arthur Schnitzler and Karl Kraus were laid to rest in the spacious Jewish section, with its special atmosphere. The Dr Karl Lueger Memorial Church, a massive Secessionist work, can be reached from the main gate (Tor 2) and is well worth a visit. There is also a precise plan of the cemetery at the main gate. The *Funeral Museum (Mon–Fri 9am–4.30pm, 1st Sat of each month 9am–4.30pm incl. guided tour | admission 7 euros | bestattungsmuseum.at)* in the chapel of rest No. 2, also offers insights into Vienna's idiosyncratic relationship with death. The Central Cemetery is also a large nature reserve, home to numerous species. *The best chance of spotting wild animals is at the Jewish cemetery, with its dense vegetation and ancient graves, some of them more than 100 years old.* Daily Nov–Feb 8am–5pm, March, Oct 7am–6pm, April–Sept 7am–7pm | Simmeringer Hauptstr. 232–244 | tram 71 Zentralfriedhof 2. Tor | Simmering | ⌕ c3

INSIDER TIP Spot the deer!

DAY TRIPS

🏞 NATIONALPARK DONAUAUEN 🦌

30km from Praterstern/ 1.5 hrs (U-Bahn and Postbus)

There is as much biodiversity here as in a rainforest. Around 100 breeding bird species share the Donauauen national park with 30 species of mammal, 10 reptile species and 60 species of fish. The park covers 90km², sits along the border with the Czech Republic and Slovakia – formerly the site of the Iron Curtain, and is one of the last undeveloped floodplains in Central Europe. It's a wonderful place to walk, cycle and enjoy nature. The National Park Centre in Orth an der Donau acts as the gateway to the park. *donauauen.at | by car: from the city boundary, Knoten Stadlau B3 via Gross-Enzersdorf to Orth (45 mins); by bus: ÖBB Post bus several times daily from U2 Aspernstrasse to Orth/Donau Schlossplatz (journey time approx. 45 mins) | ☐ d3*

🏰 STIFT KLOSTERNEUBURG
9km from Heiligenstadt/15 mins (U-Bahn and bus)

The impressive complex of Kloster-neuburg Abbey comprises medieval, Baroque and historicist elements and is located north of Vienna in the federal state of Lower Austria. Home to Augustinian monks, it is an important centre of Catholic faith. According to legend, when Margrave Leopold III wed his bride Agnes in the 12th century, her veil was carried away by the wind. Leopold managed to find it, and founded the abbey on the same spot.

Visitors are free to stroll through the vast site, explore the adjacent vineyards and orchards, and admire the archduke's emerald-encrusted hat in the treasury. The abbey runs 60- to 90-minute guided tours. You can also see the wine cellars, in a 13th-century vault, and try the produce. High-profile concerts are held occasionally (see website for details). *Daily May–Nov 9am–6pm, Dec–April 10am–4pm | admission 9 euros, day-ticket incl. guided tours & audio guide 13 euros | stift-klosterneuburg.at | by car: head north on the B14, approx. 10 mins from the city centre; by U-Bahn: U4 Heiligenstadt, then Bus 400, 402 Klosterneuburg Stiftsgarten | ⏱ 2–3 hrs | ☐ b1*

Romantics will love the beautiful Danube River landscape

EATING & DRINKING

When it comes to food, the Viennese love to indulge themselves. In fact, the city has its own cuisine, and there aren't many cities that can boast that. Traditional Viennese venues come in three different flavours: coffee house, *Beisl* and *Heuriger*. The perfect start to your sightseeing day is a visit to a traditional Viennese coffee house where you can have breakfast, read the papers at your leisure and enjoy the ambience.

At lunchtime, in the *Beisl* you can get good, inexpensive and mostly hearty Viennese cuisine. On the menu: classics such as schnitzel,

You'll find all the venues in this chapter on the pull-out map 🗺

Golden-yellow with a coat of breadcrumbs: the real Wiener Schnitzel

Knödel (dumplings), paprika chicken or stuffed cabbage rolls, at a fair price. If none of these take your fancy, you can look for Balkan and Turkish restaurants, as well as Israeli, Mexican or Vietnamese – Vienna has the same culinary offering as any other major city.

And in the evening? People take to the bars or one of the numerous *Heurigen* on the edge of the city, where wine is served not by the glass, but by the litre, and you serve yourself at the *Heuriger* buffet which offers bread with spreads, salads, sausages and bacon, dumplings and roasts.

WHERE TO EAT IN VIENNA

THURYGRUND

WÄHRING

Spitalgasse

Währinger Straße

UNI QUARTER
Here you can find anything from
a cheap breakfast to fine dining

HERNALS

MICHELBEUERN

Ottakringer Straße

Alser Straße

Lerchenfelder Gürtel

BREITENFELD

Universitätsring

Thaliastraße Ⓤ

JOSEFSTADT

Burgring

Lerchenfelder Straße

Neustiftgasse

STROZZIGRUND

Burggasse

Glacis Beisl ★ ◉
Halle Café-Restaurant ★ ◉

NEUBAU
Restaurants at every
corner – very hipster

NEUBAU

Museumsquartier Ⓤ

Phil ★ ◉

Neubaugürtel

NASCHMARKT QUARTER
A great selection of
Chinese restaurants

MARIAHILF

Kettenbrückengasse Ⓤ

Mariahilfer Gürtel

◉ Café Jelinek ★

★ **CAFÉ CENTRAL**
Splendid café that once inspired
men of letters ➤ p. 74

★ **CAFÉ JELINEK**
You can get breakfast here, even in
the evening – perfect for those who
enjoy a lie-in ➤ p. 74

★ **HALLE CAFÉ–RESTAURANT**
Trendy, unpretentious and
chic ➤ p. 76

★ **KLEINES CAFÉ**
A tiny spot in a central location,
with an idyllic garden ➤ p. 76

★ **PHIL**
Cosy café which doubles up as a
bookshop and record store ➤ p. 76

★ **VOLLPENSION**
The desserts at this trendy venue are
all baked by pensioners ➤ p. 78

★ **PLACHUTTA**
Tafelspitz and more: this place is a
stronghold of Vienna's boiled-beef
tradition ➤ p. 78

★ **ef16**
Top-quality food in a secluded courtyard
to suit the mid-range budget ➤ p. 79

★ **GLACIS BEISL**
One of the best schnitzels in town,
served in the very farthest corner of the
Museumsquartier ➤ p. 80

★ **WRENKH**
Wholesome and good: heaven for
vegetarians ➤ p. 82

HEURIGEN (WINE TAVERNS)

■1 CHRIST

His exquisite wines have made Rainer Christ one of the stars among Vienna's innovative young wine-growers. His 400-year-old family operation is an idyll with a shady garden and bower, vinotheque and delicious buffet. *Jan, March, May, July, Sept, Nov Mon–Fri 3–11pm, Sat/Sun noon–11pm; winery visit by appointment | Amtsstr. 10–14 | Jedlersdorf | tel. 01 2 92 51 52 | weingut-christ.at | tram 31 Grossjedlersdorf | bus 31A Haspinger-platz | Floridsdorf | ⊞ c1*

■2 HEURIGER HIRT

Situated atop a short but steep hill, this *Heuriger* serves enormous meat dumplings and offers a wonderful view that takes in Kahlenbergerdorf, Vienna and the Danube. *April–Oct Wed–Sun noon–10pm | Eisernenhand-gasse 8 | tel. 01 3 18 96 41 | derhirt. at | bus 400 Kahlenbergerdorf (plus 10 mins uphill on foot) | Döbling | ⊞ b1*

■3 HEURIGER OBERMANN

Family-run with a garden for guests and its own organic wines. *Thu/Fri 4–11pm, Sat 1–11pm, Sun 1–9pm | Cobenzlgasse 102 | tel. 0664 4 51 99 27 | weinbauobermann.at | bus 38A Feuerwache Grinzing | Grinzing | ⊞ b1*

■4 WEINHOF ZIMMERMANN

The wine served here comes straight from the vineyards on the hillsides surrounding this traditional tavern. Very romantic! *Mid-March–end Oct Tue–Sat 3pm–midnight, Sun noon–11pm | Mitterwurzergasse 20 | tel. 01 4 40 12 07 | weinhof-zimmermann.at | bus 39A Agnesgasse | Döbling | ⊞ C2*

■5 WEINSTÜBERL HORVATH

Cosy *Heuriger* with hearty food in a delightful quarter. In summer, you can sit outside with your glass of wine and enjoy the atmosphere. *Mon–Sat 4pm–1am, Sun 4pm–midnight | Spittelberggasse 3 | weinstueberl.at | U2, U3 Volkstheater | Neubau | ⊞ J9*

COFFEE & TEA HOUSES

■6 CAFÉ CENTRAL ★ ⚑ ☂ ♟

Luxurious café in Venetian neo-Gothic style. This is where men of letters and journalists sharpened their pens around 1900. Extremely popular with tourists – you may have to wait to be seated. *Mon–Sat 8am–9pm, Sun 10am–9pm | Herrengasse 14 | cafe central.wien | bus 1A, 2A, U3 Herrengasse | Innere Stadt | ⊞ b6*

■7 CAFÉ JELINEK ★

Rather eccentric and old-fashioned – but very authentic. In summer you can enjoy the garden, in winter a stove provides a cosy atmosphere. Want to read the papers and order a vegan breakfast at 8pm? No problem at all! *Daily 9am–10pm | Otto-Bauer-Gasse 5 | cafejelinek.steman.at | U3 Zieglergasse | Mariahilf | ⊞ J10*

■8 CAFE KORB

Pleasantly laid-back café/restaurant with a 1950s ambience that is very popular with artists. Try the

A century ago it was full of writers, today it's tourists: the famous Café Central

home-made apple strudel! Readings and concerts in the *Art Lounge* in the basement. *Mon-Sat 8am-midnight, Sun 10am-11pm | Brandstätte 9 | cafekorb.at | U1, U3 Stephansplatz | Innere Stadt | ▥ c6*

9 CAFÉ LANDTMANN ⚑

Large, classic – and admittedly expensive - café on the Ringstrasse, used by many politicians, journalists and businesspeople as a "second office". Delightful terrace in use in summer. *Daily 7.30am-10pm | Universitätsring 4 | landtmann.at | tram D, 1, 2, 37, 38, 40–44, 71, bus 1A, U2 Schottentor | Innere Stadt | ▥ a6*

10 GREGORS KONDITOREI

Can a dessert ever be a meal on its own? The cakes and pastries at Gregors Konditorei have earned the epithet "real food", and the nutty *Nusskipferl*, buttery croissants and chocolate slices – all baked to the highest standards using exclusively regional ingredients – are all extremely calorific. The breakfasts are also superb! *Tue-Sat 9am-7pm, Sun 10am-6pm | Schönbrunnerstr. 42 | tel. 01 5 44 11 27 | gregors-konditorei. at | U4 Pilgramgasse | Margareten | ▥ J11*

11 HAAS & HAAS

This traditional tea house is famous for its many types of breakfast. There is also a shop area where you can buy exquisite teas and accessories. The inner courtyard with comfortable wicker chairs is a dream. *Mon-Sat 8am-8pm, Sun 9am-6pm |*

Stephansplatz 4 | haas-haas.at | U1, U3 Stephansplatz | *Innere Stadt* | 🕮 c6

⑫ HALLE CAFÉ-RESTAURANT ★

Simple and chic, with good food. In summer, enjoy the terrace with a view of the MQ courtyard. This is a place where the in-crowd meet, with trendy exhibitions and special events in the house. *Tue noon–midnight, Wed–Sat 10am–midnight, Sun 10am–6pm | Museumsplatz 1 | diehalle.at | U1, U2, U3 Volkstheater* | *Neubau* | 🕮 a8

⑬ KAFFEE ALT WIEN

The furniture is worn, the waiters wear baggy suits and the walls are dark brown – in other words, it's a Viennese coffee house. Recommended if you're after an authentic experience. *Daily 9am–midnight | Bäckerstr. 9 | kaffee altwien.at | U1, U3 Stephansplatz | Innere Stadt* | 🕮 c6

⑭ KLEINES CAFÉ ★

A tiny, charming coffee house with cosy Chesterfield-style corner chairs and a lovely garden. You're allowed to smoke indoors here, too. Tourists seldom find their way to this café, even though a scene from *Before Sunrise*, a 1995 romantic comedy, was filmed here. *Daily 10am–2am | Franziskanerplatz 3 | U1, U3 Stephansplatz* | *Innere Stadt* | 🕮 c7

⑮ PHIL ★

The Phil is not just a well-stocked bookshop: it is also home to a café, a mini record store and a living room for

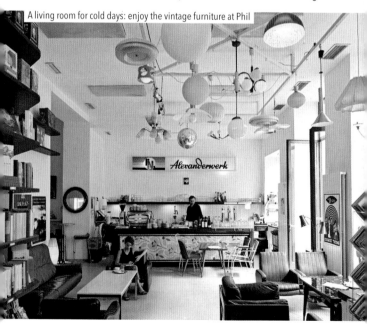

A living room for cold days: enjoy the vintage furniture at Phil

Today's Specials

Starters

FRITTATENSUPPE
Deep-fried and finely sliced egg
pancakes served in clear beef broth

GRIESSNOCKERLSUPPE
Clear beef broth with dumplings made
of semolina, milk, eggs and butter

LEBERKNÖDELSUPPE
Clear beef broth with dumplings made
of beef liver and bread

Main courses

BEUSCHEL
Finely cut offal (mainly heart and lung)
in a spicy sauce

STELZE
Grilled knuckle of pork or veal, served
with sauerkraut and bread dumplings

TAFELSPITZ
One of the best cuts of boiled beef;
usually served with shredded fried
potatoes and chive sauce or stewed
apples with horseradish

WIENER SCHNITZEL
Escalope of veal covered with
breadcrumbs and fried until
golden brown

KRAUTFLECKERLN
Noodles with spicy braised cabbage

Desserts

APFELSTRUDEL
Grated apples, nuts and raisins,
seasoned with cinnamon and sugar,
wrapped in gossamer-thin pastry sheets

KAISERSCHMARRN
Sweet dessert made from shredded
omelette, usually served with stewed
plums

PALATSCHINKEN
Sweet pancakes filled with apricot jam

POWIDLTASCHERLN
A Bohemian dessert: potato-batter
dumplings filled with plum purée

SACHERTORTE
The classic cake made of egg yolks,
sugar, a little flour and beaten egg
whites, filled with apricot jam and
covered with chocolate icing

those cold days. If you are looking for a starting point for your exploration of the 6th District (Mariahilf) and 7th District (Neubau), you are in the right place! Apart from stimulating reading, try the hearty "Philgood Breakfast": yoghurt with muesli and fruit, houmous, falafel, antipasti and pastries. *Mon 5pm–1am, Tue–Sun 9am–1am | Gumpendorfer Strasse 10–12 | tel. 01 5 81 04 89 | phil.info | U2 Museumsquartier | U1, U2, U4 Karlsplatz | Mariahilf | ⊞ a8*

INSIDER TIP
Energy for brain and body

🟦 VOLLPENSION ★

Part-time jobs to prevent poverty in old age: what started out as a pop-up project is now a trendy café. The Vollpension promises the very best pastries between Vienna and Tokyo, all baked and served by pensioners. At the weekend, come early and order the generous *"Erbschleicher"* (legacy hunter) breakfast, including cold meat and cheese, a mini cake and egg liqueur. *Mon–Fri 7.30am–10pm, Sat 9am–10pm, Sun 9am–8pm | Schleifmühlgasse 16 | vollpension. wien | U1, U2, U4 Karlsplatz | Wieden | ⊞ K10*

RESTAURANTS €€€

🟦 57 RESTAURANT

On the 57th floor of the 250m-high DC Tower, 57 promises international cuisine with regional influences. Even better than the culinary offerings are the views of the city – said to be the best in Vienna. Dress code applies. *Tue–Fri 6pm–midnight, Sat 5pm–midnight, Sun noon–3pm brunch | Donau-City-Strasse 7 | tel. 01 9 01 04 20 80 | www.fiftysevenrestaurant.at | U1 Kaisermühlen-VIC | Donaustadt | ⊞ P4*

🟦 MRAZ UND SOHN

This restaurant may be located a little off the beaten track, but it's one of the best places in town and serves food worthy of the Michelin guide. The menu is updated daily, and a 13-course tasting menu starts at 155 euros. Booking essential! *Mon–Fri 7pm–midnight | tel. 01 3 30 45 94 | Wallensteinstr. 59 | mrazundsohn.at | tram 5 Rauscherstrasse | U4 Friedensbrücke | Brigittenau | ⊞ L4*

🟦 PLACHUTTA ★

The *Tafelspitz* is superb here (and in the two branches in Hietzting and Nussdorf). Ewald Plachutta and his team serve more than a dozen different kinds of boiled beef in their chic city eatery. *Booking recommended. Daily | Wollzeile 38 | tel. 01 5 12 15 77 | plachutta.at | U3 Stubentor | Innere Stadt | ⊞ d7*

🟦 STEIRERECK

OK, even a lunch menu at Steirereck will set you back at least 100 euros; however, what you get for your money is top-level creative cuisine with a Viennese twist – such as char (a fish) from Mariazell, in beeswax accompanied by carrots, pollen and cream. *Mon–Fri 11.30am–2.30pm & from 6pm | Am Heumarkt 2a | Stadtpark | tel. 01 7 13 31 68 | steirereck.at |*

tram 2 Weihburggasse | U4 Stadtpark |
Landstrasse | ⎕ d7

21 ZUM SCHWARZEN KAMEEL

The roots of this stylish classic restaurant can be traced back to the 17th century. Chef de cuisine Sevgi Hartl's cooking is creative while still respecting tradition, and Maître Gensbichler guides his guests through the wine and cheese lists with the charm of times long past. The "Camel" also has a stand-up bar and an exquisite wine and delicatessen shop – ideal if you are looking for a culinary souvenir. *Daily 8am–midnight | Bognergasse 5 | tel. 01 5 33 81 25 | kameel.at | U3 Herrengasse | Innere Stadt | ⎕ b6*

RESTAURANTS €€

22 AUX GAZELLES

The essence of the Orient for all the senses: the glamorous combination of brasserie, café and deli with an oyster bar, tea salon and club. It even has a Moroccan steam bath! *Café and restaurant Tue–Sat 10am–midnight, club with DJ Fri/Sat 8pm–4am, hamam & salon de thé Tue–Fri noon–8pm, Sat 11am–8pm | Rahlgasse 5 | tel. 01 5 85 66 45 | auxgazelles.at | bus 57A, U2 Museumsquartier | Mariahilf | ⎕ a8*

23 BEOGRAD

They say that Vienna is where the Balkans begin – and at this place you can believe it, with food as hearty and portions as huge as anything you can find further south. There is nearly always live music here too. *Tue–Sat*

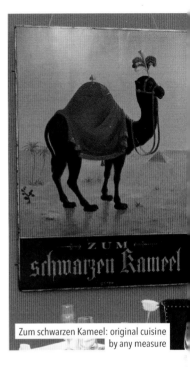

Zum schwarzen Kameel: original cuisine by any measure

5–10.30pm | Schikanedergasse 7 | tel. 01 5 87 74 44 | restaurant-beograd.at | U4 Kettenbrückengasse | Wieden | ⎕ K10

24 EF16 ★

This small restaurant occupies a fairy-tale courtyard that has frequently been proclaimed the most beautiful outdoor dining area in the city. The food is international and prepared to the highest standards, but the prices are well below Michelin levels. Ask the friendly staff for recommendations and be surprised! *Mon–Sat 5.30–11pm | Fleischmarkt 16 | tel. 01 5 13 23 18 | ef16.at | U1, U4 Schwedenplatz | Innere Stadt | ⎕ c6*

25 FIGLMÜLLER ⚑

People wait in long queues here for a schnitzel. But they are worth the wait: huge, wafer-thin and particularly tender. Booking essential! There is another branch nearby *(Bäckerstrasse 6). Daily 11am–9.30pm | Wollzeile 5 | tel. 01 5 12 6177 | figlmueller.at | U1, U3 Stephansplatz | Innere Stadt | � d6*

26 GLACIS BEISL ★ ⚑

This well-hidden restaurant in the rear courtyard of the Museumsquartier serves original Austrian cuisine and one of the best schnit-

INSIDER TIP
Welcome shade

zels in town. On hot summer days, the plants make the inner courtyard into an oasis. At Christmastime, even the mulled wine here is specially prepared in small quantities. *Tue 5pm–midnight, Wed–Sun noon–midnight | Museumsplatz 1 | tel. 01 5265660 | glacisbeisl.at | U2, U3 Volkstheater | Neubau | ⊞ a8*

27 GMOAKELLER

Sophisticated and refined home-style cooking using traditional recipes with a touch of the Styria region, in the atmosphere of a cosy pub. Excellent wines. *Mon–Sat 11am–midnight | Am Heumarkt 25 | tel. 01 7 12 53 10 | gmoakeller.at | U4 Stadtpark | Landstrasse | ⊞ d8*

28 HANSEN

Wonderful restaurant in the cellar of the stock exchange, with plenty of green plants adding to the ambience. Modern, light cuisine. *Mon–Fri 9am–9pm, Sat 9am–3pm | Wipplinger-str. 34 | tel. 01 5 32 05 42 10 | hansen. co.at | tram D, 1, 71 Börse | U2 Schottentor | Innere Stadt | ⊞ b5*

29 HEUER AM KARLSPLATZ

This place is pretty fancy, with pickles in enormous preserving jars, unusual dishes such as grilled octopus with smoked black pudding, and home-made lemonade. Everything is local and organic, and there's an art gallery in the building. *Tue–Sat from 6pm | Treitlstr. 2 | tel. 01 8 90 0590 | heuer-amkarlsplatz.com | U1, U2, U4 Karlsplatz | Wieden | ⊞ b8*

30 HUTH

Elegant high-quality Viennese cuisine and fine wines, served in a stylish space in a cellar. *Daily noon–11pm | Schellinggasse 5 | tel. 01 5 13 56 44 | huth-gastwirtschaft.at | tram 2, D Weihburggasse | Innere Stadt | ⊞ c7*

31 MOCHI

Japanese cuisine meets Tel Aviv and Berlin. The results include exciting crossover dishes such as grilled aspar-agus with miso butter. Booking recommended. *Mon–Sat 11.30am–10pm | Praterstr. 15 | tel. 01 9 25 13 89 | mochi.at | U1, U4 Schwedenplatz | Leopoldstadt | ⊞ d5*

32 NATURKOST ST JOSEF

It may look like meat, but it's not. At this venue all the food is organic and vegetarian, and most of it is vegan. The lunchtime buffet can win over even the most committed of carni-vores. On weekdays there are vegan, gluten-free and nut-free lunchtime

Treat yourself to a schnitzel at the Figlmüller, provided there is no queue!

options. Afterwards, you can get the best coffee in the nearby Zollergasse, with its many cosy cafés. *Closed evenings & Sun | Mondscheingasse 10 | tel. 01 5 26 68 18 | U3 Neubaugasse | FB: Naturkost St. Josef |* Neubau | ⌑ H9

33 PLUTZER BRÄU

This rustic restaurant serves hearty Austrian fare, including vegetarian options. They also offer home-brewed beer and an extensive wine list. *Mon-Fri 4pm-midnight, Sat/Sun 11.30am-midnight | Schrankgasse 2/ corner Stiftgasse | tel. 01 5 26 12 15 | plutzerbraeu.at | U2, U3 Volkstheater |* Neubau | ⌑ J9

34 RAMIEN

This pioneer among Vienna's modern Asian restaurants is highly praised for its unpretentious styling and wonderful cooking and has remained a favourite place for the city's young creative crowd. Fantastic noodle soups, rice dishes with tofu, duck, salmon and shrimps. *Tue-Sun 11am-midnight | Gumpendorfer Str. 9 | tel. 01 5854798 | ramien.at | U2, U4 Karlsplatz |* Mariahilf | ⌑ a8

35 REBHUHN

Lovely pub with wood panelling and classic Austrian cuisine. Dish of the day followed by an apricot dumpling? *Daily 11.30am-10.30pm, summer*

Sat/Sun 6.30–10.30pm | Berggasse 24 | rebhuhn.at | tel. 01 3 19 50 58 | tram D Schlickgasse | *Alsergrund* | ◻ K6

36 SCHILLING

From fried chicken and schnitzel to *Tafelspitz* and *Kaiserschmarrn* with *Zwetschgenröster*, this place serves traditional Viennese fare in a cosy setting. Booking recommended. *Daily 11.30am–10pm | Burggasse 103 | tel. 01 5 24 17 75 | schilling-wirt.at | U6 Burggasse-Stadthalle | Neubau | ◻ G9*

37 STEMAN

In some countries, checked tablecloths are synonymous with traditional cuisine; in Vienna, it's wood-panelled walls. The cosy Steman serves everything that traditional Viennese cuisine has to offer, from goulash and roast beef with fried onions to schnitzel and *Kaiserschmarrn* – sometimes with a modern twist. Booking essential! *Mon–Sat 11am–11pm | Otto-Bauer-Gasse 7 | tel. 01 5 97 85 09 | steman.at | U3 Zieglergasse | Mariahilf | ◻ H10*

38 UBL

This is not the place to come if you are counting calories, but it is perfect for fans of classic Austrian specialities such as schnitzel, knuckle of pork or fried offal served in a really relaxed inn with a round iron stove, old wooden panelling and floorboards. *Wed–Sun noon–2pm, 6pm–midnight | Pressgasse 26 | tel. 01 5 87 64 37 | U4 Kettenbrückengasse | Wieden | ◻ K10*

39 WRENKH ★

Vienna's master of healthy cuisine and a mecca for vegetarians. It's a fashionable spot with a chic bar, a shop for "functional food" and cooking classes. *Mon–Fri 11am–11pm, Sat noon–11pm | Bauernmarkt 10 | tel. 01 5331526 | wrenkh-wien.at | U1, U3 Stephansplatz | Innere Stadt | ◻ c6*

RESTAURANTS €

40 BITZINGER 🐷

The *Wurst* stall behind the Staatsoper is obviously not a restaurant in the normal meaning of the word. However, you cannot eat sausages in greater style in Vienna than at *"beim Bitzinger"*, and they even serve champagne to go with your food. In addition, they are open almost around the clock. Even Mick Jagger has visited. There is another branch in the Prater. *Daily | between the Oper and Albertina | tel. 0681 84 23 14 74 | bitzinger-wien.at | bus 59A, tram D, 1, 2, 62, 65, 71, U1, U2, U4 Karlsplatz | Innere Stadt | ◻ b7*

41 DER WIENER DEEWAN

Only the well-mannered should eat here, since it's up to the diner to decide how much they want to pay for the fresh daily selection of fruity and spicy Indo-Pakistani stews and curries. Make sure that you leave some space for the marvellous *suji halwa* dessert, which is spiced with cardamom. If you're too stingy, then you run the risk of a frosty reception

> **INSIDER TIP**
> Addictive semolina

The marvellous team at vegetarian restaurant Wrenkh

on your next visit! *Mon–Sat 11am–11pm | Liechtensteinstr. 10 | tel. 01 9 25 11 85 | deewan.at | tram D, 1, 37, 38, 40–44, 71, U2 Schottentor | Alsergrund | ▥ a5*

42 GREEN DOOR BISTRO

Located in the basement of the Nationalbibliothek and appreciated by students, public servants and bankers. Its style resembles that of a designer restaurant with bistro cuisine, but the prices are surprisingly moderate. There are daily menus (both meat and vegetarian) as well as vegan options. *Mon–Fri 11am–3pm | Am Josefsplatz 1, access from the Burggarten, to the left of the butterfly house | tel. 0677 64 39 47 16 | green-door.at | U2 Museumsquartier, bus 2A Michaelerplatz | Innere Stadt | ▥ b7*

43 INIGO

Cheerful, laid-back meeting place for everyone. The vegetarian meals and inexpensive set lunch are something special. *Mon–Fri 10am–11pm | Bäckerstr. 18 | tel. 5 12 7451 | inigo.at | U3 Stubentor | Innere Stadt | ▥ d6*

44 KÄUZCHEN

The most entertaining menu in Vienna, decorated with cartoons and featuring dishes with original names such as "Simone de Beauvoir" (schnitzel cordon bleu with camembert and cranberries). Dishes range from

Austrian to vegan. Last orders one hour before closing time. *Mon–Sat 4pm–2am, Sun 4pm–midnight | Gardegasse 8 | tel. 01 5 24 78 82 | kaeuzchen.at | U2, U3 Volkstheater | Neubau | J9*

45 KOLAR BEISL

In the centre of the Old Town but hidden away: the Kolar Beisl prepares wonderfully hearty flatbreads from the wood-fired grill until 1am, served with quark, egg or sour cream, ham and mushrooms. *Mon–Sat 11am–1am, Sun 1pm–1am | Kleeblattgasse 5 | tel. 01 5 33 52 25 | kolar-beisl.at | bus 2A, 3A Brandstätte | U1, U3 Stephansplatz | Innere Stadt | b6*

46 MASCHU MASCHU

Falafel? At the Maschu Maschu! Their delicious Asian cuisine is served at two central outlets – the other branch is on the Innere Stadt *(Rabensteig 8 | U1, U4 Schwedenplatz | L7)*. The food comes as pittas, tortillas and in bowls. *Daily 11.30am–midnight | Neubaugasse 20 | tel. 01 9 90 47 13 | maschu-maschu.at | bus 13A, U3 Neubaugasse | Neubau | H9*

47 SCHWEIZERHAUS ⚑

An institution in the Wurstelprater. Hearty old-school Viennese specialities, from schnitzel and silver carp to knuckle of pork and goulash. When the weather is fine, you can sit outside in the shade of enormous chestnut trees. *Daily mid-March–end Oct 11am–11pm | Prater 116 | tel. 01 7 28 01 520 | schweizerhaus.at | U1 Messe Prater | Leopoldstadt | O7*

48 SIEBENSTERN-BRÄU

Apart from hearty Austrian dishes such as beef goulash with dumplings, this basement restaurant with a courtyard garden also offers home-brewed beer. At weekends, from 11am to 3pm, there are reasonably priced lunchtime menus (including a vegan option). What about a hemp or chilli beer to go with it? *Sun–Tue 11am–9pm, Wed–Sat 11am–10pm | Siebensterngasse 19 | tel. 01 5 23 86 97 | 7stern.at | tram 49 Stiftgasse | U2, U3 Volkstheater | Neubau | J9*

> **INSIDER TIP**
> **Schnitzel meets hemp**

49 TIROLERGARTEN

Hearty alpine cooking in a Tyrolean farmhouse with a pleasant garden? You don't need to drive out to the mountains to enjoy it – only as far as the Schönbrunn Zoo grounds in Hietzing. Dishes range from bacon and bread, *Schlutzkrapfen* (noodles stuffed with spinach and curd cheese) and organic beef goulash, to spinach and Tyrolean dumplings. *Daily 11am–6.30pm | Schlosspark Schönbrunn | tel. 01 8 79 35 560 | zoovienna-gastro.at | U4 Hietzing, then bus 56A, 56B or 58A | Hietzing | b2*

50 TOFU & CHILI

In recent years, numerous Asian restaurants have opened around the Naschmarkt. Tofu & Chili serves authentic northern Chinese cuisine. Here, the noodles are hand-pulled and served in a

> **INSIDER TIP**
> **Hand-pulled noodles**

Schweizerhaus (Swiss House) beer garden serves old-style Viennese cuisine

wok or in soup. Of course, you can order tofu with chilli sauce as well. If you would prefer to eat out in the sun, just order a lunch box to take away. *Mon–Sat 11.30am–10pm | Linke Wienzeile 18 | tel. 01 5 85 69 70 | U1, U2, U4 Karlsplatz | Mariahilf | ⬚ b8*

51 TÜRKIS

Fast food – but of high quality. The family-run Türkis does one of the best kebabs in town as well as vegetarian dishes. The delicious meat skewers are available at 16 outlets, including at Hauptbahnhof station. *Daily | Hauptbahnhof Wien, ground floor | tel. 01 6 00 50 10 | tuerkis.at | U1 Hauptbahnhof | Favoriten | ⬚ c2*

52 WALDVIERTLER HOF

A typical country inn – in the heart of town! Substantial specialities from northern Lower Austria, friendly service and a cosy, rustic atmosphere, plus a large garden with chestnut trees. There are reasonably priced set lunches. *Mon–Sat 11am–11pm | Schönbrunner Str. 20 | tel. 01 5 86 35 12 | waldviertlerhof.at | U4, bus 59A Kettenbrückengasse | Margareten | ⬚ J10*

SHOPPING

Vienna can be expensive, but it doesn't have to be. Luxury shoppers will find their eldorado in the "Golden Quarter" or on Kärntner Strasse. In general, the expensive and often long-established shops are in the historic centre.

A number of young designers have opened small boutiques selling fashion, furniture and jewellery in the 6th and 7th districts, and these are particularly common around Neubaugasse and Lindengasse. If you are more interested in classical souvenirs, Augarten porcelain and the legendary *Sachertorte* are always a good choice.

You'll find all the venues in this chapter on the pull-out map 🗺

Sacher Confiserie: a chocolate lover's paradise

Things are more down-to-earth and sensual at Vienna's almost two dozen food markets; the most interesting is the spacious Naschmarkt. A flea market is held next to it every Saturday. Many shops do not close their doors until 7pm or 8pm during the week. However, shopping still stops at 6pm – at the latest – on Saturday. Most shops are closed on Sunday; even groceries can only be bought at a few shops at railway stations.

WHERE TO SHOP IN VIENNA

WÄHRING

THURYGRUND

Jörgerstraße

Ottakringer Straße

ROSSAU

Spitalgasse

Währinger Straße

Alser Straße

Trachten Tostmann ★ ◉

BREITENFELD

MARIAHILFER STRASSE

The side streets of this shopping mile are also worth exploring

JOSEFSTADT

Julius Meinl am Graben ★ ◉

Altmann & Kühne ★ ◉

Stephansplatz

Lerchenfelder Straße

Neustiftgasse

ALTLERCHENFELD

Burggasse

Burgring

Ⓤ Burggasse-Stadthalle

◉ Ina Kent ★

SPITTELBERG

Opernring

Neubaugürtel

◉ Naschmarkt ★

Mariahilfer Straße

Kettenbrückengasse

Ⓤ Westbahnhof

MARIAHILF

Ⓤ

Rechte Wienzeile

NASCHMARKT AREA

Saturday flea market and small shops in the 4th District

LAIMGRUBE

Igramgasse Ⓤ

Mariahilfer Gürtel

Favoritenstraße

Wiedner Hauptstraße

FÜNFHAUS

Linke Wienzeile

MARGARETEN

MARCO POLO HIGHLIGHTS

★ **INA KENT**
Hip leather handbags for the fashion-conscious ➤ p. 90

★ **JULIUS MEINL AM GRABEN**
Vienna's best delicatessen, with delicacies from all over the world ➤ p. 92

★ **AUGARTEN**
Vienna's world-famous porcelain figures are produced by Europe's second-oldest manufacturer of fine china ➤ p. 93

★ **NASCHMARKT**
Bazaar atmosphere at Vienna's largest and most fascinating food market ➤ p. 94

★ **TRACHTEN TOSTMANN**
Buy or hire traditional clothes to look like a true Austrian ➤ p. 96

★ **ALTMANN & KÜHNE**
Beautifully packaged chocolates and other treats for those with a sweet tooth ➤ p. 97

GRABEN, KÄRNTNER STRASSE
Flagship stores for luxury brands

LANDSTRASSER HAUPTSTRASSE
Shopping centre and the place to pick up practical items

Augarten

● Augarten (Palais Augarten) ★

LEOPOLDSTADT

INNERE STADT

WEISSGERBER

Park Prater

Stadtpark

Belvederegarten

LANDSTRASSE

ERDBERG

500 m
547 yd

ACCESSORIES, JEWELLERY & HANDICRAFTS

1 ANNA STEIN

Unusual souvenirs and knick-knacks – from felt purses and art cards to Brazilian jewellery. The atmosphere is like a salon, and the pavement café is a welcome extra. *Kettenbrückengasse 21 | tel. 0699 12 03 14 30 | FB: Anna Stein Salon | U4 Kettenbrückengasse | Margareten | ⮂ K10*

2 FREY WILLE

Elegant, decorative enamel jewellery with 24-carat gold decoration. *Lobkowitzplatz 1 | tram D, 1, 2, 71, U1, U2, U4 Karlsplatz | ⮂ K8; Stephansplatz 5 | shop.freywille.com | U1, U3 Stephansplatz | Innere Stadt | ⮂ b7*

WHERE TO START?

Vienna's central shopping area is located around the **Stephansdom** *(⮂ c6)*. The Graben and Kohlmarkt are lined with exquisite boutiques as are (but less so) Rotenturmstrasse and Kärntner Strasse. It is considerably less expensive on the big peripheral shopping stretches of Landstrasser Hauptstrasse, Wiedner Hauptstrasse, Favoritenstrasse and especially Mariahilfer Strasse. There are also many interesting and unusual shops in the side streets in the city centre and around the Naschmarkt.

3 HORN

Accessories and leather travel goods, timelessly elegant and perfectly crafted. *Bräunerstr. 7 | rhorns.com | U1, U3 Stephansplatz | ⮂ K8; Mahlerstr. 5 | U1, U2, U4 Karlsplatz | Innere Stadt | ⮂ b7*

4 INA KENT ★

Hand-made leather bags in many colours. Hard-wearing and popular accessories among the fashion-conscious in Vienna. The bags are both aesthetically pleasing and functional, and suitable for storing tablets or laptops. *Neubaugasse 34 | inakent.com | U3 Neubaugasse | Neubau | ⮂ H9*

5 JAROSINSKI & VAUGOIN SILBERSCHMIEDE

All that glitters here admittedly comes with a price tag to match – but the bowls, cutlery and candlesticks produced by the oldest silver manufacturer in the country are well worth a look, even if you aren't buying. *Zieglergasse 24 | vaugoin.com | U3 Zieglergasse | Neubau | ⮂ H9*

6 KAUFHAUS SCHIEPEK

Glamorous necklaces, earrings and accessories created by professional designers, together with beads and equipment for you to make your own at home. *Teinfaltstr. 3 | kaufhaus-schiepek.com | tram D, 1, 71 Burgtheater | U3 Herrengasse | Innere Stadt | ⮂ b6*

7 NEW ONE

Lots of bling, but with style: the filigree earrings and necklaces and glittering bracelets on sale here strike a balance between timelessness and change. The modern range produced by the traditional jeweller Schullin is designed to appeal to a younger clientele. *Goldschmiedgasse 10 | newoneshop.com | U1, U3 Stephansplatz | Innere Stadt | ⠶ c6*

Enamel rings by Frey Wille, with 24-carat gold

8 SKREIN
A young team of excellent artistic jewellers present their own creations and those of well-known colleagues. Extremely innovative and individual. *Spiegelgasse 5 | skrein.at | U1, U3 Stephansplatz | Innere Stadt | ⠶ c7*

9 SLAVIK
A high-quality jewellery selection featuring creations by international contemporary artists displayed in sophisticated surroundings. *Himmelpfortgasse 17 | galerie-slavik.com | U1, U3 Stephansplatz | Innere Stadt | ⠶ c7*

10 WALTER WEISS
Hundreds of hand-made hair and clothes brushes that will last forever. *Mariahilfer Str. 33 | walterweisse.at | bus 13A Stiftgasse | U3 Neubaugasse | Mariahilf | ⠶ a8*

ANTIQUES & ANTIQUARIAN BOOKSHOPS

11 DER BUCHFREUND
Vienna's biggest antiquarian bookshop and university bookstore in a central location. Whether you are interested in art, philosophy, children's books or esoteric titles – you can find everything here. Browse the catalogue online in advance. *Sonnenfelsgasse 4 | buchschaden.at | U1, U4 Schwedenplatz | Innere Stadt | ⠶ c6*

12 DOROTHEUM
You can buy all kinds of furniture, fine china, books, jewellery, paintings, toys and curios – at all price and quality levels – in this more than 300-year-old auction house, either at auction or in the "free sales" section. Wandering through the building and poking around is always worthwhile. *Dorotheergasse 17 | dorotheum.com | U1, U3 Stephansplatz | Innere Stadt | ⠶ b7*

13 INLIBRIS GILHOFER NFG.
One of the top addresses for typical Austrian objects, with autographs, old prints and books. *Rathausstr. 19 | inlibris.com | tram D, 1, 37, 38, 40–44, 71 | U2 Schottentor | Innere Stadt | ⠶ J7*

14 KOVACEK
The place to look for premium-quality antique glassware. *Spiegelgasse 12 | kovacek.at | bus 2A, U1, U3 Stephansplatz | Innere Stadt | ⠶ b7*

DELICATESSENS, TEA & WINE

15 BABETTE'S

Very pleasant mixture of international cookery books and exotic herbs and spices. Also cookery lessons and spice workshops. *Schleifmühlgasse 17 | babettes.at | U4 Kettenbrückengasse | Wieden | ⊞ K10; Am Hof 13 | U3 Herrengasse | Innere Stadt | ⊞ K7*

16 BE(E) HONEY WELTHONIG

Sweet selection of honey specialities from all over the world, including Vienna (feel free to taste them!), plus skincare products – all containing honey, of course. *Hainburger Str. 68-70 | welthonig.at | U3 Kardinal Nagl Platz | Erdberg | ⊞ O9*

17 JULIUS MEINL AM GRABEN ★

The best delicatessen in town. In addition to the fabulous selection of fine foodstuffs (including around 400 different cheeses), the three floors also have room for a restaurant and café, as well as a wine and sushi bar. *Graben 19 | meinlamgraben.at | bus 1A, 2A, U1, U3 Herrengasse | Innere Stadt | ⊞ b6*

18 SCHÖNBICHLER

Vienna's best tea specialist has more than 100 varieties from all over the world – from noble classics to modern mixtures in cool aluminium tins. *Wollzeile 4 | bus 3A, U1, U3 Stephansplatz | Innere Stadt | ⊞ c6*

19 TEE UND GESCHENKE

If you're still hunting for the perfect souvenir, then you'll find something here, especially if you're looking for food-related items such as the famous Zaunerstollen from Bad Ischl, a delicious nougat-like treat, made with crushed wafers, hazelnuts, chocolate and more. *Zieglergasse 4 | teeundgeschenke.at | U3 Zieglergasse | Neubau | ⊞ H10*

INSIDER TIP
Sliced delight

20 THE WINE REBELLION

A small but friendly wine store with a bar, offering predominantly organic Austrian wines. They also serve toast with unusual toppings: how about sliced salmon trout with sorrel? *Wine store Tue-Fri noon-7pm, Sat 2-7pm, bar Thu-Sun 6pm-midnight | Burggasse 36 | thewinerebellion.at | U2, U3 Volkstheater | Neubau | ⊞ H9*

FILMS, PHOTOGRAPHY, GAMES, MUSIC & BOOKS

21 DAMAGE UNLIMITED GAMES CENTER

Games for children and adults, with Vienna's largest selection of board games. *Theobaldgasse 20 | U2 Museumsquartier | U3 Neubaugasse | Mariahilf | ⊞ a8*

22 DOBLINGER

Traditional shop for old and new sheet music as well as specialist literature and recordings. *Dorotheergasse 10 | doblinger.at | U1, U3 Stephansplatz | Innere Stadt | ⊞ b7*

23 HARTLIEBS BÜCHER

It is always best to buy books from

From precious crystal chandeliers to vases: Lobmeyr is Vienna's glass specialist

people who love to read. Petra Hartlieb is such a woman: the author and bookseller even wrote the bestseller *Meine wundervolle Buchhandlung* (My Wonderful Bookshop). *Porzellangasse 36 | hartliebs.at | tram D Seegasse | U4 Rossauer Lände | Alsergrund | ⬜ J6*

INSIDER TIP For the love of printed paper

24 SUBSTANCE

Tens of thousands of vinyl records – from 1980s classics to the latest Indie releases. *Westbahnstr. 16 | substance-store.com | tram 49, U3 Zieglergasse | Neubau | ⬜ H9*

25 UNITED CAMERA

New and second-hand cameras: if you can't find what you are looking for in this friendly shop, there are several other photo shops in this street.

Westbahnstr. 23 | united-camera.at | tram 49 Zieglergasse, U6 Burggasse–Stadthalle | Neubau | ⬜ H9

ARTS & CRAFTS, DESIGN & FURNITURE

26 AUGARTEN ★ ▶

The filigree figures and china from Europe's second-oldest porcelain manufacturer are some of Vienna's most popular souvenirs. You can see how they are made in an hour-long tour of the headquarters in Augarten Palace, and you can buy the products in the flagship store in the city too. *Guided tours Mon–Thu 10.15am & 11.30am, Thu also 2pm & 3.30pm | admission 19 euros | Obere Augartenstr. 1 | U2 Taborstrasse | Leopoldstadt | ⬜ L6; flagship store: Spiegelgasse 3 | augarten.com | U1, U2 Stephansplatz | Innere Stadt | ⬜ L5*

⁷ LOBMEYR

Exquisite crystal chandeliers, mirrors, glassware. The Glass Museum on the second floor is well worth visiting – and free. *Kärntner Str. 26 | lobmeyr.at | U1, U3 Stephansplatz | Innere Stadt | ⌂ c7*

²⁸ MAUERER HÜTE

The best place for headwear from Panama hats to wool berets. This specialist shop, which was founded in 1873, has a large selection of ladies' and gentlemen's hats by various brands. Its signature hat is the Mauerer Porpkye, a round hat with a narrow brim. *Mariahilfer Str. 117 | hut-online.at | U3 Zieglergasse | Mariahilf | ⌂ H10*

²⁹ MODE WIEN

A curious mixture of home accessories, fashion and original souvenirs, all of which are unique items or made in small quantities by local up-and-coming designers. *Bauernmarkt 8 | modewien.at | U1, U3 Stephansplatz | Innere Stadt | ⌂ c6*

³⁰ RÉPERTOIRE

A design store whose wares fall under the category of "things that nobody needs, but everybody wants" – from quirky notebooks to lamps and origami animal heads. *Otto-Bauer-Gasse 9 & 18 | repertoire.at | U3 Zieglergasse | Mariahilf | ⌂ H10*

³¹ WOKA LAMPS VIENNA

Art Nouveau and Art Deco lamps made to designs by Josef Hoffmann, Adolf Loos, Kolo Moser and others. *Singerstr. 16 | woka.com | U1, U3 Stephansplatz | Innere Stadt | ⌂ c7*

MARKETS

³² BRUNNENMARKT ⚑

After visiting Vienna's biggest street market in the multicultural area of Ottakring, it is really relaxing to stop at one of the many restaurants on Yppenplatz with tables outside. Try the wonderful Turkish sweets at *Kamelya Café (Brunnengasse 74)* which is open daily until 11pm. Market *Mon–Fri 6am–9pm, Sat 6am–5pm, gastro stalls Mon–Sat 6am–11pm | Brunnengasse/ Yppenplatz | tram 44 Yppengasse | U6 Josefstädter Strasse | Ottakring | ⌂ G8*

> **INSIDER TIP**
> **Turkish sweets**

³³ NASCHMARKT ★ ⚑

Known as "Vienna's belly", the largest and most charming food market in the city exudes the cheerful, lively atmosphere of a bazaar. Especially charming are the dealers from the Balkans and Turkey, who praise their wares at the top of their voices – and even give free samples! *Mon–Fri 6am–9pm, Sat 6am–6pm | between Kettenbrücken-gasse & Karlsplatz on the Wienzeile | U1, U2, U4 Karlsplatz | U4 Kettenbrückengasse | Mariahilf | ⌂ K9–10*

FASHION

³⁴ FLO VINTAGE

"Antiques with stitches" is the motto of Ingrid Raab's boutique for vintage clothes. More than 5,000 items, from

Delicious, fresh and healthy: wonderful fruit in the Naschmarkt

1920s Charleston dresses to 1950s New Look outfits, as well as silk stockings, model hats, costume jewellery and much more. Film stars and trend scouts like to rummage around in the shop. *Schleifmühlgasse 15a | flovintage.com | U4 Kettenbrückengasse | Wieden | ☐ K10*

🟥 FREITAG

Bags and rucksacks by this Swiss cult label are made out of old truck tarpaulins. The handles are strips of safety belts, and old bike tubes are used for the seams. There are some 1,600 models in all colours of the rainbow in the heart of Vienna's hippest shopping district. *Neubaugasse 26 | freitag.ch | U3 Neubaugasse | Neubau | ☐ H9*

🟥 GREEN GROUND

Would you like to shop sustainably and still be fashionable? There doesn't have to be a contradiction: this concept store sells eco-friendly and socially responsible fashion with style. *Closed Mon | Porzellangasse 14–16 | greenground.at | tram D Bauernfeldplatz | Alsergrund | ☐ J6*

🟥 HENNY ABRAHAM

Exquisite, unique articles brought together from the four corners of the globe: from saris and kimonos, kilims and quilts, to mother-of-pearl cutlery and rice paper. *Closed Mon | Schleifmühlgasse 13 | U4 Kettenbrückengasse | Wieden | ☐ K10*

38 LAMBERT HOFER JUNIOR

In case you still need something to wear for your evening at the Staatsoper or the Musikverein, you can hire costumes and evening wear here. *Margaretenstr. 25 | tel. 01 5 87 44 44 | lambert-hofer.at | U4 Kettenbrückengasse | Wieden | ⚏ J12*

39 LE MIROIR

A dreamy boutique selling enchanting clothes by young French designers. *Closed Mon | Strobachgasse 2 | lemiroirwien.com | U4 Pilgramgasse | Margareten | ⚏ K11*

40 LILA

If you have experimental tastes and love angular cuts, colourful fabrics and oversized skirts, then you can't go wrong with the two Lila shops. Lisi Lang's idiosyncratic creations don't fit in with any fashion era that we can think of. *Kirchengasse 7 | tram 49 Kirchengasse | Neubau | ⚏ J9; Westbahnstrasse 3 | shop.ila.cx | tram 49 Westbahnstrasse/Neubaugasse | U3 Neubaugasse | Neubau | ⚏ H9*

41 PARK

Avant-garde fashion and 1980s cult wear, unusual accessories, international fashion magazines and exclusive furniture on two floors near Mariahilfer Strasse. *Mondscheingasse 20 | U3 Neubaugasse | Neubau | ⚏ H9*

42 POLYKLAMOTT

Just a few metres from the flea market, Polyklamott has vintage clothing and second-hand cashmere sweaters in good condition and at low prices. If you happen to have lost your sunglasses or gloves, the 24-hour vintage vending machine outside the shop may be able to assist in an emergency. Make sure that you bring five 1-euro coins! *Mollardgasse 13 | polyklamott.at | U4 Kettenbrückengasse | Mariahilf | ⚏ J10*

INSIDER TIP
A helpful machine

43 SCHELLA KANN

Extravagantly modern couture for women with a fuller figure: functional, straightforward, made of luxurious fabrics and – usually – in dazzling colours. *Spiegelgasse 15 | schellakann.com | U1, U3 Stephansplatz | Innere Stadt | ⚏ c7*

44 STEFFL

Lifestyle items and fashion at this seven-floor traditional department store are exquisite and expensive. An external panorama lift takes you to the restaurant with a rooftop terrace and wonderful views over the inner city. *Kärntner Str. 19 | steffl-vienna.at | U1, U3 Stephansplatz | Innere Stadt | ⚏ c7*

45 TRACHTEN TOSTMANN ★

Genuine traditional clothing for all the family, for hire as well as for sale. The family-run business manufactures its clothes in Upper Austria and Vienna. If you prefer a unique garment, they will create one for you. *Schottengasse 3a | tostmann.at | tram D, 1, 37, 38, 40–44, 71, U2 Schottentor | Innere Stadt | ⚏ a6*

Delightful! Fabulous sweets adorned with pink ribbons by Demel confectionery

CONFECTIONERY

46 ALTMANN & KÜHNE ★

For those with a discerning sweet tooth: bonbons and mini-chocolates delightfully boxed in the shape of a heart or a book. *Graben 30 | altmann-kuehne.at | bus 1A, 2A, U1, U3 Stephansplatz | Innere Stadt | ⊞ c6*

47 DEMEL ⚑

Superior boxes of chocolates and cakes from the former confectioner to the imperial court. *Kohlmarkt 14 | demel.at | bus 1A, 2A | U3 Herrengasse | Innere Stadt | ⊞ b6*

48 MANNER SHOP ⚑

The classic nougat wafers in pink wrapping are sold fresh every day in the flagship store – also available in wholemeal, lemon or coconut. *Stephansplatz 7 | U1, U3 Stephansplatz | Innere Stadt | ⊞ c6*

49 SACHER CONFISERIE ⚑

Here you can buy the world-famous cake to take home with you or have it shipped anywhere in the world. *Kärntner Str. 38 | sacher.com | tram D, 1, 2, 71, U1, U2, U4 Karlsplatz | Innere Stadt | ⊞ c7*

50 SCHOKO COMPANY

You will find an enormous selection of wines, liqueurs, honey, coffee and chocolate here – all organic, regional and fair trade. Styrian chocolate manufacturer Zotter promises unusual and ever-new flavours. Why not try its fish-flavoured chocolate or Firewood Brandy chocolate? *Naschmarkt 326–331 | schoko company.at | U1, U2, U4 Karlsplatz | Mariahilf | ⊞ K9*

INSIDER TIP
Chocolate with a fishy taste

51 XOCOLAT

A temple of chocolate in the Palais Ferstel arcade, where some of the tasty treats have been hand-made in-house and the rest are imported from all over the world. *Freyung 2 | xocolat.at | bus 1A, 2A, U3 Herrengasse | Innere Stadt | ⊞ b6*

NIGHT LIFE

The Austrian capital has become something of an underground hotspot among fans of late-night clubbing and partying.

The thud of electronic beats has even been heard emanating from the world-famous Burgtheater recently. While Vienna may be best known for its classical music, Boys' Choir and opera – with a club scene lagging far behind that of Berlin, Paris or London – for the last decade or so the city has been flirting heavily with electronic music, and the scene is increasingly making inroads into traditional cultural institutions.

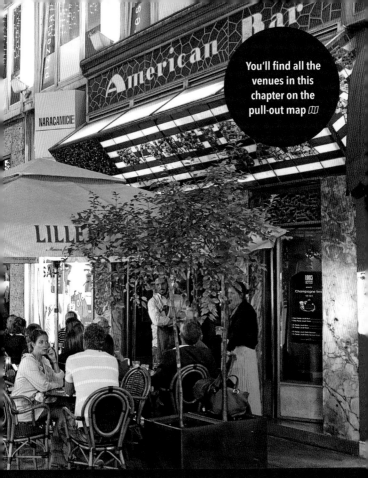

You'll find all the venues in this chapter on the pull-out map 🗺

The 1st District has many places where you can sit outside

With more than two million visitors, the Donauinselfest (Danube Island Festival), held annually in June, is one of the world's biggest festivals (admission free). And for those who prefer to keep things quiet and low key, the city has also acquired a good selection of stylish wine and cocktail bars in recent years. Live music is staged every night in the many small bars and cafés under the so-called *Gürtelbögen* – the series of railway arches underneath the U6 railway line.

GOING OUT IN VIENNA

Grelle Forelle ★

OBERDÖBLING

Billrothstraße

Albert-Stifter-Str.

Jägerstraße

Spitelauer Lände

Brigittenauer Lände

Nussdorfer Straße

Obere Donaustraße

Rossauer Lände

ALSERGRUND

Währinger Gürtel

Gentzgasse

Währinger Straße

WÄHRING

Spitalgasse

U-BAHN ARCHES
Cult restaurants
along the U6

Flex ★

Schottenring

Alser Straße

Schottenring

Alser Straße

Lerchen-felder Gürtel

JOSEFSTADT

Josefstädter Straße

Burgtheater ★

Theater in der Josefstadt ★

INNERE STADT

Thaliastraße

Volksgarten Disco und Pavillon ★

Neustiftgasse

Burgring

NEAR
MARIAHILFER STRASSE
Great (music) bars in
the side lanes

Staatsoper ★

Opernring

Neubaugürtel

Burggasse

Museumsquartier

Musikverein ★

Westbahnhof

Mariahilfer-Straße

Karlsplatz

Rechte Wienzeile

MAGD
GRUN

U4 ★

MARCO POLO HIGHLIGHTS

★ **FLEX**
Concerts and clubbing: high-decibel "in" spot in a bunker next to the U-Bahn ➤ p. 102

★ **GRELLE FORELLE**
Stylish underground club ➤ p. 105

★ **U4**
Dance where Falco used to celebrate ➤ p. 105

★ **VOLKSGARTEN DISCO UND PAVILLON**
Stylish techno and electro parties in a garden with a pool ➤ p. 106

★ **MUSIKVEREIN**
Probably the world's best acoustics: classical music performances at the highest level ➤ p. 108

★ **STAATSOPER**
The embodiment of Austrian musical culture ➤ p. 109

★ **BURGTHEATER**
An iconic venue and the flagship of German-language theatre ➤ p. 110

★ **THEATER IN DER JOSEFSTADT**
Theatre for the intelligentsia, with innovative contemporary plays ➤ p. 111

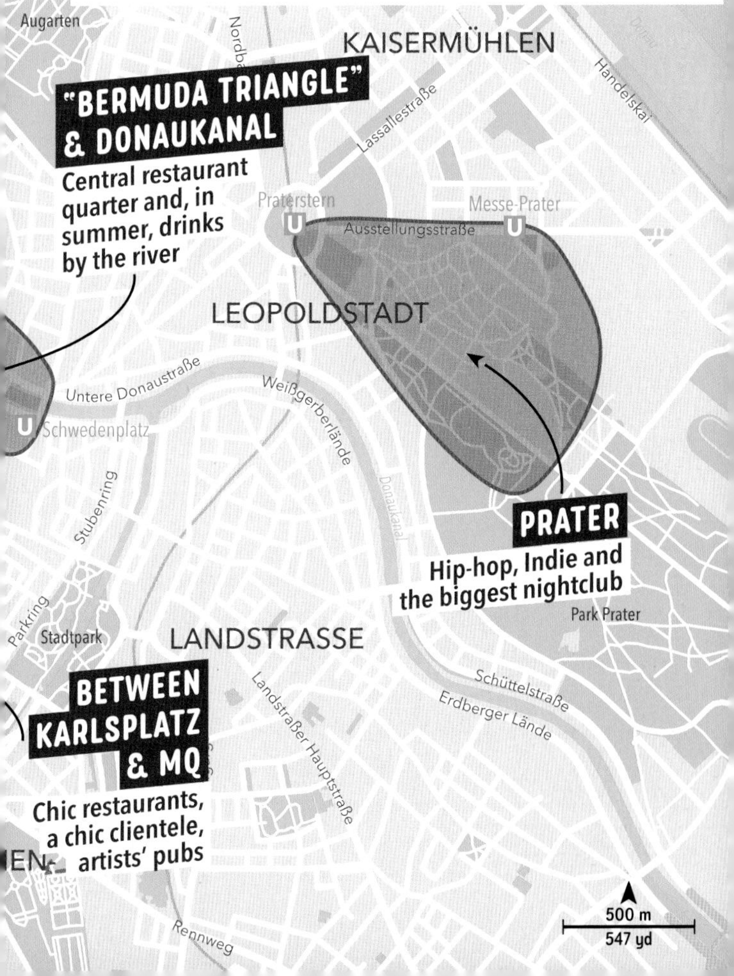

Augarten

Nordba

KAISERMÜHLEN

Dui

Handelskai

Lassallestraße

"BERMUDA TRIANGLE" & DONAUKANAL
Central restaurant quarter and, in summer, drinks by the river

Praterstern Ⓤ

Messe-Prater Ⓤ

Ausstellungsstraße

LEOPOLDSTADT

Untere Donaustraße

Weißgerberlände

Ⓤ Schwedenplatz

Stubenring

Donaukanal

PRATER
Hip-hop, Indie and the biggest nightclub

Park Prater

Parking

Stadtpark

LANDSTRASSE

Landstraßer Hauptstraße

Schüttelstraße

Erdberger Lände

BETWEEN KARLSPLATZ & MQ
Chic restaurants, a chic clientele, IEN_ artists' pubs

Rennweg

▲
500 m
547 yd

BARS & MUSIC PUBS

1 ARENA

Time-honoured alternative stage for everything from oldie rock and punk to reggae and techno. *Baumgasse 80 | arena.wien | bus 80A, U3 Erdberg | Landstrasse | ▥ P11*

2 CAFÉ EUROPA

If your feet are aching from too much shopping on Mariahilfer Strasse, treat yourself to lunch at this trendy venue or sample one of its many home-made lemonades. In the evening, this charmingly relaxed café transforms into a bar. *Daily 9am–5am (kitchen 9am–4am) | Zollergasse 8 | cafeeuropa. at | U3 Neubaugasse | Neubau | ▥ J9*

3 CHELSEA

Rock, house, Brit and Indie pop – full, loud, great DJs and many live concerts.

Football matches, including the English Premier League, are shown on big screens – the club is called Chelsea after all. *Mon–Sat 6pm–4am, Sun 4pm–3am | U-Bahn-bogen 29–30/Lerchenfelder Gürtel | chelsea.co.at | U6 Thaliastrasse | Josefs tadt | ▥ G8.*

4 DACHBODEN

The terrace at this bar has spectacular views over Vienna at sunset, and every Friday night there is a line-up of DJs. *Daily 3pm–1am | Lerchenfelder Str. 1–3 | dachbodenwien.at | U2, U3 Volkstheater | Neubau | ▥ J8*

5 ESPRESSO

A charming 1950s bar that – contrary to its name – specialises in liqueurs such as herbal bitters and gin rather than coffee. *Mon–Fri 9am–midnight, closed Sat in summer | Burggasse 57 | espresso-wien.at | U2, U3 Volkstheater | Neubau | ▥ H9*

6 FLEX ★

Underground in a bunker next to the U-Bahn: this place is for lovers of pandemonium – drum 'n' bass, noise, jungle, hardcore. *Mon–Sat 7pm–1am | Donaukanalpromenade/Augarten-brücke | flex.at | U2, U4 Schottenring | Innere Stadt | ▥ c5*

7 FLUC + FLUC WANNE

A pioneer of the party scene, for dancing or just listening. Also quirky art performances. *Mon–Sat 8pm–4am | Praterstern 5 | fluc.at | U1, U2 Praterstern | Leopoldstadt | ▥ N6*

Listen up, people: there's a sunset to be seen on Dachboden's terrace!

8 HALBESTADT

American bar that's low on chic but serves wonderful long drinks. The location underneath the U-Bahn arches creates a special atmosphere. Outside restaurant in summer: what Austrians call a Schanigarten. *Wed–Sat 7pm–1am | U-Bahnbogen 155, opposite Währinger Gürtel 146 | halbestadt.at | U6 Nussdorfer Strasse | Alsergrund | ▥ H5*

9 LOOSBAR

Tiny American bar where – besides stunning the *fin de siècle* architecture – the list of cocktails is unique. *Daily noon–4am | Kärntner Durchgang 10 | loosbar.at | U1, U3 Stephansplatz | Innere Stadt | ▥ c7*

10 MIRANDA BAR

Half chic, half hipster, with a colour scheme borrowed from Miami Vice and a cocktail list you'd find at a holiday resort. *Mon–Wed 6pm–midnight, Thu–Sat 6pm–1am | Esterhazygasse 12 | miranda-bar.com | U3 Zieglergasse | bus 13A Magdalenenstrasse | Mariahilf | ▥ J10*

11 O – DER KLUB

A large club on several floors, with electro DJs every Friday and 1990s party hits every Saturday. Admission from 13 euros. *Passage Opernring/Operngasse | FB: o der klub | U1, U2, U4 Karlsplatz | Innere Stadt | ▥ b8*

12 PLANTER'S CLUB

The extravagantly decorated bar with an old-school colonial feel has a gigantic selection of drinks. You can fortify yourself next door in the *Livingstone* with exotic Californian specialities before you start imbibing! *Planter's Club Mon–Thu 5pm–2am, Fri/Sat 5pm–3am, Livingstone Mon–Sat 5pm–midnight | Zelinkagasse 4 |*

plantersclub.com | tram 1, U2, U4 Schottenring | Innere Stadt | *b5*

13 PORGY & BESS

Ambitious international programme for jazz fans – live gigs almost every night. On most Mondays from 7pm to 8pm, the *Strenge Kammer*, a small secondary stage, becomes a venue for musical experimentation, readings and exhibitions. *Daily from approx. 7.30pm | Riemergasse 11 | porgy.at | U3 Stubentor | Innere Stadt | d7*

INSIDER TIP
Away from the mainstream

14 ROBERTOS BAR

A plush and cosy American bar with a healthy dose of bling and an enormous chandelier that fills the entire venue. The delicious cocktails are equally glamorous. *Daily 7pm–4am | Bauernmarkt 11 | robertosbar.at | U1, U3 Stephansplatz | Innere Stadt | c6*

15 SZENE WIEN

Concerts from experimental to rock music – usually in the "hard" department: punk, rock, techno or rave. *Hauffgasse 26 | szene.wien | U3 Enkplatz | Simmering | c2*

16 TANZCAFÉ JENSEITS

This former brothel is now a cosy yet louche bar that attracts a thirty-something crowd for plenty of dancing and flirting. *July/Aug Wed–Sat 8pm–4am, Sept–June Tue–Sat 8pm–4am | Nelkengasse 3 | tanzcafe-jenseits.com | U3 Neubaugasse | Mariahilf | J10*

CLUBS & DISCOS

17 CLUB ROXY

Red leather and red lights – there's a lot of grooving going on in this 1960s-style bar. A key address for fans of soul, funk, R'n'B and hip-hop. *Fri/Sat 11pm–4am | Faulmanngasse 2/Operngasse | roxyclub.org | tram 62,*

The atmosphere in the plush Tanzcafé Jenseits is designed to facilitate flirting!

65, U1, U2, U4 Karlsplatz | Wieden | ▥ b8

18 DONAU

Formerly home to a synagogue, this venue are now a popular destination for techno fans. Watch out though: the entrance to the club is easy to miss. *Mon–Thu 8pm–4am, Fri/Sat 8pm–6am, Sun 8pm–2am | Karl-Schweighofer-Gasse 10 | donautechno.com | tram 49 Stiftgasse | U2 Museumsquartier | Neubau | ▥ a8*

19 GRELLE FORELLE ★

The only large-scale underground club in Vienna that plays cool electronic music – always with a sense of style and a cast of top international DJs. On two floors with an area of 1,000m². *Fri/Sat 11pm–6am | Spittelauer Lände 12 | grelleforelle.com | U4, U6 Spittelau | Alsergrund | ▥ J4*

20 PASSAGE

One of the top dance palaces. Here, under the Burgring in the cool atmosphere of Babenberger Passage, top DJs play house, dance floor, R'n'B and much more. *Thu–Sat 11pm–6am | Burgring 3 | club-passage.at | tram D, 1, 2, 71 Burgring | U2 Museumsquartier | Innere Stadt | ▥ b8*

21 PRATERDOME

A pure party atmosphere reigns supreme at Austria's biggest disco, which boasts a spacious dancefloor and a hugely varied playlist. *Fri/Sat 10pm–6am | Riesenradplatz 7 | prater dome.at | U1 Praterstern | Leopoldstadt | ▥ N6*

22 PRATERSAUNA

You'll often find people here dancing to electro, house and techno in bikinis and board shorts, as during the summer this stylish club with its large garden and pool transforms into a beach club. *Opening hours depend on the programme | Waldsteingartenstr. 135 | pratersauna.tv | U2 Messe | Leopoldstadt | ▥ O7*

23 SASS

The party doesn't really get going at this stylish after-hours club until everywhere else has closed. *Thu/Fri 11pm–6am, Sat 11pm–5am, Sun 6–11am | Karlsplatz 1 | sassvienna.com | U1, U2, U4 Karlsplatz | Innere Stadt | ▥ c8*

24 U4 ★

A legendary club where the city's first-ever gay party was held. Falco, who was a regular, performed his debut single "Ganz Wien" here. Past excesses have since calmed, and today DJs play a large variety of different musical styles: Tuesday is student night, Wednesday 1990s hits, Thursday club music, Friday rock, and Saturdays are themed. *Tue–Sat 10pm–6am | admission 10 euros | Schönbrunner Str. 222 | u4.at | U4 Meidling Hauptstrasse | Meidling | ▥ F12*

25 VIE I PEE

Make sure you spruce yourself up when you come here, as the bouncers at Vienna's brand-new and only hip-hop club are very strict. *Wed, Fri/Sat 11pm–6am | Waldsteingartenstr. 135 | vieipee.com | U2 Messe-Prater | Leopoldstadt | ▥ O7*

26 VILLAGE BAR

Chic and popular gay bar with a good selection of drinks, a video wall, free WiFi and air conditioning. *Sun–Thu 8pm–2am, Fri/Sat 8pm–3am | Stiegengasse 8 | village-bar.at | U4 Kettenbrückengasse | Mariahilf | ⌑ J10*

27 VOLKSGARTEN DISCO UND PAVILLON ★

Beautiful people and great atmosphere. During the summer, the party moves outside into the large garden, which even has a pool (though no swimming allowed). The romantic small tables among the shrubs and flowers are a hotspot for flirting. *Disco all year round Thu–Sat 10pm–6am, pavilion (outdoors) April–Sept daily*

Watch movies on a big screen at the Gartenbaukino

11am–2am, clubbing Thu–Sat 10pm–6am | Burggarten 1 | volksgarten.at | tram D, 1, 46, 49, U2, U3 Volkstheater | Innere Stadt | ⌑ a7

CABARET & SMALL THEATRES

28 KULISSE

The pioneer theatre for all kinds of cabaret with a message is located in an old suburban pub – food and drinks are served during performances. *Rosensteingasse 39 | tel. 01 4 85 3 8 70 | kulisse.at | tram 2, 9 Mayssengasse | tram 43 Rosensteingasse | Hernals | ⌑ F7*

29 NIEDERMAIR

Small theatre where many satirists celebrated their first successes and where stars also like to appear. *Lenaugasse 1A | tel. 01 4 08 44 92 | niedermair.at | tram 2, U2 Rathaus | Josefstadt | ⌑ J8*

30 STADTSAAL

Cabaret theatre seating 360. This is where stars and promising talents appear; also international guest performers. Performances (almost) every evening. *Mariahilfer Str. 81 | tel. 01 9 09 22 44 | stadtsaal.com | U3 Neubaugasse | Mariahilf | ⌑ H10*

31 WUK

Independent studio and culture house with music and dance performances, concerts, readings and exhibitions. *Währinger Str. 59 | tel. 01 40 12 10 | wuk.at | tram 5, 33, 37, 38, 40–42, U6 Volksoper | Alsergrund | ⌑ H6*

CINEMAS

You can see many interesting films in open-air cinemas during the warm summer months *(incl. arena.co.at, kinowienochmie.at, kinoamdach.at and volxkino.at)*.

32 BREITENSEER LICHTSPIELE

The Breitenseer Lichtspiele is a real gem. An alternative to the mainstream, it shows documentaries, arthouse films and Austrian classics. The venue is possibly the oldest cinema in the world in continuous use: films have been shown here since 1905 – and the Breitenseer Lichtspiele is proud of this. In order to make sure that things stay this way, support this cinema by buying a ticket for a special event: a silent film with live piano accompaniment (once a month at a weekend, see website for dates). *Breitenseer Str. 21 | tel. 01 9 82 21 73 | bsl-wien.at | tram 49 | U3 Hütteldorfer Strasse | Penzing | ⊞ D10*

INSIDER TIP
Sunday performance

33 CINEMAGIC 👯

A special cinema for young film fans from the age of three. All kinds of films are shown – from funny cartoons to prize-winning productions for older kids and teenagers. The highlight is the annual International Children's Film Festival in mid-November, which takes place at three cinemas. *Uraniastr. 1 | tel. 01 4 00 08 34 00 | cinemagic.at | tram 1, 2 Julius-Raab-Platz | U1, U4 Schwedenplatz | Innere Stadt | ⊞ M7*

34 FILMMUSEUM ☂

A cineaste's mecca: celluloid rarities from around the world. *Augustinerstr. 1 | tel. 01 5 33 70 54 | filmmuseum.at | tram D, 1, 2, U1, U2, U4 Karlsplatz | Innere Stadt | ⊞ b7*

35 GARTENBAUKINO

This cinema features premieres in original language with subtitles. Versatile programme and a big screen. *Parkring 12 | gartenbaukino.at | tel. 01 5 12 23 54 | tram 2, 71, D, U3 Stubentor | Innere Stadt | ⊞ d7*

36 TOP KINO

An independent cinema with a discerning programme, which also functions as a popular restaurant. À la carte breakfast is served every Sunday with a reduced admission fee of 3.20 euros for the lunchtime film! *Kitchen & top bar Mon–Wed 11am–midnight, Thu–Sat 11am–1am, Sun 10.30am–midnight | Rahlgasse 1 | tel. 01 2 08 30 00 | topkino.at | bus 57A Rahlgasse | U1, U2 Museumsquartier | Mariahilf | ⊞ a8*

INSIDER TIP
Cinema, comedy & piano

37 VOTIVKINO 👯

Independent cinema with a café, showing many films in the original language with subtitles. Special event: baby cinema every other Tuesday between 11am and noon (babies up to 12 months old). The room is not fully darkened, the sound is a little softer than usual and there is a nappy-changing table.

INSIDER TIP
Sleep tight, baby!

Those who are asked to perform at the Staatsoper have made it to the top!

Währinger Strasse 12 | tel. 01 3 17 3 5 71 | votivkino.at | tram D, 1, 37, 38, 40-44, 71, U2 Schottentor | Alsergrund | ⌑ a5

CONCERTS

🟥 KONZERTHAUS

The dazzlingly white Art Nouveau building is a stronghold of modern classics – Mahler, Bartók, Stravinsky – as well as contemporary music. There are also regular performances of all other musical styles from Baroque to Renaissance and from pop to jazz, in the various halls. The Vienna Symphony is this institution's in-house orchestra. *Lothringer Str. 20 | tel. 01 242002 | konzerthaus.at | tram D, 71, U4 Stadtpark | Landstrasse | ⌑ d8*

🟥 KURSALON

Good solid performances of melodies in waltz time by Lanner, Strauss and the like take place in this pleasure pavilion on the edge of the Stadtpark. *Johannesgasse 33 | ticket hotline 01 5 12 5790 | kursalonwien.at | tram 2, U4 Stadtpark | Landstrasse | ⌑ d7*

🟥 MUSIKVEREIN ⭐

The main concert hall, the Golden Hall, has probably the finest acoustics in the world and has hosted all the major stars, ranging from Bruckner, Mahler and Strauss to Karajan, in the last 130 years or so. It remains a bastion of the classical tradition to this day. As the home of the Vienna Philharmonic Orchestra, it regularly welcomes the most famous international orchestras, conductors and soloists. Four small ultra-modern halls in the cellar. *Musikvereinsplatz 1 | tel. 01 5 05 81 90 | musikverein.at | tram D, 1, 2, 62, 71, U1, U2, U4 Karlsplatz | Innere Stadt | ▥ c8*

41 RADIO-KULTURHAUS

Innovative culture centre in the home of the former Austrian national radio broadcaster. There are concerts featuring all kinds of music, plus readings, discussions and so on in the main studio on most days. *Argentinierstr. 30a | tel. 01 50 17 03 77 | radiokultur haus.orf.at | U1 Taubstummengasse | Wieden | ▥ L10*

OPERA, OPERETTA & MUSICALS

42 L.E.O.

Mini-versions of Verdi, Puccini and the like for two soloists plus piano, with the audience as the choir, in the "Letzten Erfreulichen Operntheater" (Last Satisfying Opera Theatre) – Viennese cabaret art with tremendous charm! *Ungargasse 18 | theater leo.at | U4 Landstrasse/Wien Mitte | Landstrasse | ▥ M9*

43 RAIMUNDTHEATER

Operettas were produced here for decades, but today musicals such as *Beauty and the Beast* or *Phantom of the Opera* are staged here. *Wallgasse 18–20 | tickets 01 5 88 85 | musical vienna.at | tram 6, 18, U6 Gumpendorfer Str. | Mariahilf | ▥ G11*

44 RONACHER

Musicals, variety and guest musical performances in this beautifully renovated variety theatre in the Belle Époque style. *Seilerstätte 9 | tickets 01 58 88 51 11 | musicalvienna.at | U1, U3 Stephansplatz | Innere Stadt | ▥ c7*

45 STAATSOPER ★

The State Opera – the "House on the Ringstrasse" – symbolises Vienna's position as a music metropolis in a way that can only be matched by the

GOLDEN VOICES: THE VIENNA BOYS' CHOIR

The "Wiener Sängerknaben" performs every Sunday from mid-September through to the end of June, and on Christmas Day, in the chapel of the *Hofburg (access from Schweizerhof | Innere Stadt | ▥ b7)*, where they sing with the male choir of the Staatsoper and the Vienna Philharmonic. Concerts begin at 9.15am. Order your tickets via the *Hofmusikkapelle (tel. 01 5 33 99 27 | hofmusikkapelle.gv.at or culturall. com/ticket/hmk)*. You can also experience the Vienna Boys' Choir at the much acclaimed *Konzertsaal für Musik und Theater (MuTh) (Am Augartenspitz 1 | tel. 01 3 47 80 80 | muth.at, info at wsk.at | U2 Taborstrasse | Leopoldstadt | ▥ L6)*. Its acoustics are marvellous. This venue also hosts rock and jazz concerts, as well as other cultural events.

Musikverein. Since its opening in 1869, almost all the world's greatest opera singers have appeared on its stage and the most famous conductors have led the Vienna Philharmonic, the State Opera's orchestra. A different opera is performed almost every day during the 10 months of the season – from 1 September to 30 June. Ticket prices range from 2 euros (standing) to 287 euros. To avoid queuing for hours, it is advisable to book tickets in advance from the *Bundestheaterverband* (Federal Theatre Association) in writing (see p. 148). You can possibly buy tickets shortly before performances from ticket agencies. The tent erected on the rooftop terrace which is used for operas for children is extremely successful.

INSIDER TIP
Grand opera for free

In warmer weather (April, May, June and Sept), but not during the summer break, free opera performances are shown live on a big screen at the eastern side of the building. *Opernring 2 | tel. 01 51 44 40 | staatsoper.at | bus 59A, tram D, 1, 2, 62, 65, 71, U1, U2, U4 Karlsplatz | Innere Stadt | ⊞ b8*

46 THEATER AN DER WIEN

The first performance of Beethoven's *Fidelio* took place in this theatre, which opened its doors in 1801. Plays by Kleist, Grillparzer, Raimund and Nestroy, as well as operettas by Strauss, Suppé, Millöcker, Zeller, Lehár, Kálmán and others, were also premiered here. For some years now, it has been operating once again as a year-round opera house. *Linke Wienzeile 6 | tel. 01 5 88 85 | theater-wien.at | U4 Kettenbrückengasse | U1, U2, U4 Karlsplatz | Mariahilf | ⊞ b8*

47 VOLKSOPER

The "little" sister of the State Opera specialises in light operas, operettas and the occasional musical; the quality of the performances is almost as high. *Währinger Str. 78 | tel. 01 51 44 40 | volksoper.at | tram 40–42, U6 Währinger Strasse/Volksoper | Alsergrund | ⊞ H6*

48 WIENER KAMMEROPER

The Wiener Kammeroper is famous for its unconventional productions featuring unknown singers. In the summer months, the troupe moves to the palace theatre at Schloss Schönbrunn. *Fleischmarkt 24 | tel. 01 5 88 85 | theater-wien.at | bus 2A, U4 Schwedenplatz | Innere Stadt | ⊞ d6; Schönbrunner Schlosstheater | tel. 01 8 12 50 04 0 | tram 58, U4 Schönbrunn | Hietzing | ⊞ D–E12*

THEATRE

49 AKADEMIETHEATER

This offshoot of the Burgtheater shares the same ensemble as its big brother and presents mainly 20th-century classics and contemporary drama. *Lisztstr. 1 | tel. 01 5 14 44 45 45 | burgtheater.at | tram D, 2 Schwarzenbergplatz | U4 Stadtpark | Landstrasse | ⊞ d8*

50 BURGTHEATER ★ ⚑

The flagship of German-language theatre has sometimes found itself at the

You become a part of the spectacle at the glamorous Burgtheater

centre of controversy: during the Claus Peymann era (1989–99), and more recently, when the judiciary had to deal with a financial scandal. Martin Kušej, who previously managed the Residenztheater in Munich, has been the theatre's artistic director since the 2019/20 season. The theatre still guarantees performances of classic and modern plays of the highest standard. There is also a good bookshop in the foyer. *Universitätsring 2 | tel. 01 51 44 40 | burgtheater.at | tram D, 1, 71, U3 Herrengasse | Innere Stadt | ⊞ a6*

⑤ THEATER IN DER JOSEFSTADT ★

This stronghold of light drama and comedy, with occasional forays into classic and modern drama, is becoming increasingly daring with more innovative works and productions. *Josefstädter Str. 26 | tel. 01 42 70 03 00 | josefstadt.org | tram 2 Lederergasse | bus 13A Theater in der Josefstadt | U2 Rathaus | Josefstadt | ⊞ H8*

⑤ VIENNA ENGLISH THEATRE

This small, but excellent, theatre presents first-rate light comedies and some classic plays – in English, of course. *Josefsgasse 12 | tel. 01 40 21 26 00 | englishtheatre.at | tram 2, U2 Rathaus | Josefstadt | ⊞ J8*

⑤ VOLKSTHEATER

Traditional theatre with a broad repertoire, large ensemble and socio-critical attitude. *Arthur-Schnitzler-Platz 1 | tel. 01 52 11 10 | volkstheater.at | U2, U3 Volkstheater | Neubau | ⊞ a7*

ACTIVE & RELAXED

The Badeschiff at the Donaukanal is a hotspot in summer

SPORT & WELLNESS

In summer, when half the city is covered in lush green, the Viennese go to the Prater or Donauinsel, slacklines are put up and frisbees are thrown. During colder months, people play sport indoors.

HIKING 🐗
Vienna and hiking go well together. There are 240km of trails through and around the city. You can find maps on the Stadt Wien app. A popular hiking trail with great views is the *Stadtwanderweg 1 (start and finish at tram D, Nußdorf, Beethovengang)*: it leads through vineyards to Kahlenberg, Vienna's highest point.

INSIDER TIP
On the edge The *Rundumadum* trail goes around the entire city.

INDOOR SPORT 🏸
Badminton, volleyball, basketball, table tennis, soccer and table football are on offer at the three 🐗 *Sports & Fun* halls operated by the city of Vienna *(daily | admission 4 euros | wien.gv.at/freizeit/sportamt/sport staetten)*. You can play tennis or squash at *Club Danube (clubdanube. at)* and boulder at *Edelweiss-Center (edelweiss-center.at), Boulderbar (boulderbar.net)* or *Blockfabrik (block fabrik.at)*.

JOGGING
The 4.4km-long Hauptallee in the Prater *(sport-oesterreich.at/prater-hauptallee | U1, U2 Praterstern)* and the paths on the 21km-long Danube island *(wien.gv.at/umwelt/gewaesser/ donauinsel | depending on the area U1 Donauinsel, U2 Donaustadtbrücke, U6 Neue Donau)*, as well as the Stadtpark, Türkenschanzpark and Schönbrunn Palace Park, are especially popular with joggers and Nordic walkers *(info: runningcheckpoint.at)*.

Autumn runs are a delight in Schönbrunn Palace Park

OUTDOOR CLIMBING

Have you ever climbed an old anti-aircraft artillery tower? You can do this at the 34m-high wall in the 6th District (flakturm-klettern.at | U3 Neubaugasse). If you prefer climbing in parks, you can choose from three options: the *high-rope climbing park at the Gänsehäufel (hochseilklettergarten.at)*, the *Danube Island climbing park (kletterpark-donauinsel.at)* and the *Waldseilpark Kahlenberg (erlebniswelt-kahlenberg.at | bus 38 A Elisabethwiese)*, where you balance on rope bridges at heights of up to 20m, traverse nets and swing from tree to tree.

SPAS

If you are in need of recuperation, visit the modern *Therme Wien (daily 9am–10pm | admission from 24 euros | Kurbadstr. 14 | thermewien.at | U1 Oberlaa)*. Here, at the city's south-eastern edge, solariums, saunas, scent grottos, gyms, beauty salons and an extensive pool landscape will make you feel much better.

WATER SPORTS

Where is the best place to enjoy the summer weather? By the water! Right by U-Bahn line 1 is the idyllic *Alte Donau (alte-donau.info | U1 Alte Donau)*, a charmingly old-fashioned leisure area with beaches, boats for hire and cosy pubs. At the end of Alte Donau is a wakeboard lift *(Am Wehr 1 | wakeboardlift.at)*, where you can also take a course. Next to the U1 stop Alte Donau, the Viennese have fun at the *Hofbauer Sailing School (An der oberen Alten Donau 186 | hofbauer.at)*, which also offers stand-up paddling. At the *Marina Wien (Handelskai 343 | danubesurfer.com)*, close to the U2 station Donaumarina, you can wakesurf Hawaiian style.

FESTIVALS & EVENTS

JANUARY–EARLY MARCH

New Year's Concert (1 Jan): The Vienna Philharmonic perform in the Golden Hall of the Musikverein (□ c8). Internet lottery for tickets in Feb, nearly a year in advance (!), at *wiener philharmoniker.at*

Carnival and ball season: More than 200 festive balls in spectacular settings.

Resonanzen (second half Jan): Festival of old music. *Konzerthaus | ticket hotline 01 24 20 02 | konzert haus.at | □ c8*

Refugee Ball (end Feb/early March): All are welcome. The proceeds go to the Wiener Integrationshaus. *Rathaus | tickets: wien-ticket.at | fluechtlings ball.at | □ a6*

MARCH–MAY

Oster-Klang (Holy Week/Easter weekend): Top-class musicians including the Vienna Philharmonic play solemn and festive works *(ticket hotline 01 5 88 85)*.

Easter Market: Around 60 exhibitors present arts and crafts, Easter decorations and culinary wares at Schloss Schönbrunn. *ostermarkt.co.at | □ D–E12*

Spring Festival: Held in the *Konzerthaus* or the *Musikverein. Ticket hotline. 01 24 20 02 | konzert haus.at | □ c8*

APRIL–JUNE

Vienna City Marathon: Race from Reichsbrücke to Heldenplatz. *Tel. 01 6 06 95 10 | vienna-marathon.com*

Wiener Festwochen: Cutting-edge theatre from around the world performed at dozens of locations. *Lehárgasse 11 | tel. 01 58 92 20 | festwochen.at*

Donauinselfest (end June): Europe's biggest open-air music festival takes place over three days, and also

10 stages and 18 tents: the Donauinselfest mega party

features sport and cabaret. 🐷 Admission is free. *donauinselfest. at* | *⊞ O–P5*

JULY–SEPTEMBER

Jazzfest (early July): Held in the streets, clubs and the Staatsoper. *Ticket hotline 01 7 12 42 24 | vienna jazz.org* | *⊞ b8*

ImPulsTanz – Vienna International Dance Festival (early July–mid-Aug): Contemporary avant-garde dance from all over the world. *Ticket hotline 01 5 23 55 58 39 | impulstanz.com*

🐷 **Filmfestival am Rathausplatz**: Opera and operetta performances and recorded concerts on a big screen. *filmfestival-rathausplatz.at* | *⊞ a6*

🐷 **Popfest** (end July): Established bands and newcomers play in front of Karlskirche over three days. *Admission free | popfest.at* | *⊞ c8*

OCTOBER

Lange Nacht der Museen: 90 museums open until 1am, all accessible with a single ticket.

Viennale: International film festival. *Tel. 01 52 6 59 47 69 | viennale.at*

Wien Modern (end Oct–end Nov): Music of the 20th and 21st centuries at the Musikverein *(⊞ c8)* and Konzerthaus *(⊞ c8)*. *Tel. 01 24 20 02 & 01 5 05 81 90 | wienmodern.at*

NOVEMBER/DECEMBER

Christmas Markets: numerous locations.

Silvesterpfad (31 Dec): New Year's Eve Trail, with stalls, stages and dance tents in the city centre. Highlight: when the Pummerin bell in St Stephen's rings in the New Year *(⊞ c6)*. *silvesterpfad.at*

SLEEP WELL

HOME FROM HOME

Charity begins at home at *Magdas (85 rooms | Ungargasse 38 | tel. 01 7 20 02 88 | magdas-hotel.at | U3 Rochusgasse | € | Landstraße | ⅢM9).* Formerly a priests' home, the building is now run as a non-profit hotel where refugees are trained for jobs in the hotel trade. The hotel's upcycling is chic and there is a garden and an organic, mainly vegetarian, fair-trade restaurant that serves a few meat dishes as well. Close by: the Stadtpark, inner city and Belvedere Palace. The hotel has interesting offers on its website. If you come by train or bicycle, you may get a discount.

INDUSTRIAL ROMANTIC

The Gegenbauer family enterprise not only produces vinegar – it has also converted the first floor of its factory into a hotel called *Wiener Gäste Zimmer (10 rooms | Waldgasse 3 | tel. 01 6 04 10 88 | gegenbauer.at | bus 14A Wielandplatz | U1 Keplerplatz | €€ | Favoriten | Ⅲ c2),* which contains five romantic rooms laid out in an industrially influenced design. Breakfast is put together using only ingredients produced by the company, including coffee from the in-house roastery, as well as honey, bread and home-pressed apple juice. Make sure you sign up for a tour of the factory too!

A BEACH IN THE CITY 👥

This friendly family hotel *Strandhotel Alte Donau (29 rooms | Wagramer Str. 51 | tel. 01 2 04 40 40 | strand hotel-alte-donau.at | U1 Alte Donau | € | Donaustadt | Ⅲ Q2)* on the edge of the Alte Donau recreation area is only a few minutes from the city cen-tre by U-Bahn. Private beach with

Are you dreaming of your own shop? The Grätzlhotel will make it come true!

lawns for sunbathing. Children welcome!

EAT NEXT DOOR

Schreiners Gastwirtschaft (5 rooms | Westbahnstr. 42 | tel. 0676 4 75 40 60 | schreiners.cc | U6 Burggasse-Stadthalle | €€ | Neubau | ⊞ H9) is an idyllic green oasis in the centre of Vienna. Here, you don't just enjoy excellent food, but also stay overnight next door to the pub in rooms with a balcony or terrace. The entire operation is "overseen" by the pub's "guard dog"!

A COMFORTABLE TRAILER

In the garden of *Hotel Daniel (116 rooms | Landstraßer Gürtel 5 | tel. 01 90 13 10 | hoteldaniel.com | tram D, U 1 Hauptbahnhof | €€ | Landstraße | ⊞ M11)* is a silver 1950s trailer that has been fitted with a bath tub, basin, air-conditioning, heating, TV and WiFi.

You can book the 16-m² trailer for a comfortable stay.

CHECK OUT THE NEIGHBOURHOOD

"Grätzl" is the name of a Viennese neighbourhood. At the *Grätzlhotel (contact: Urbanauts Hospitality GmbH | tel. 01 2 08 39 04 | graetzl hotel.com | €€)* former business premises have been turned into accommodation. Explore four lively quarters of the city: on Meidlinger Markt in Meidling *(⊞ b2)*, on Karmelitermarkt in Leopoldstadt *(⊞ L7)*, in the Karolinenviertel near Belvedere Palace *(⊞ L11)* and in the Servitenviertel in Porzellangasse *(⊞ J6)*. Your neighbours aren't going to be other hotel guests, but bars and cafés, restaurants and shops.

DISCOVERY TOURS

Do you want to get under the skin of the city? Then these discovery tours provide the perfect guide. They include advice on which sights to visit, tips on where to stop for that perfect holiday snap, a choice of the best places to eat and drink and suggestions for fun activities.

The Museumsquartier offers plenty of spaces to recover from an overdose of art

DISCOVERY TOURS OVERVIEW

Kahlenberg
▲ 484

Kahlenberg &
Leopoldsberg

4

Döbling

Sieveringer Str.

Gersthofer Str.

Hernals

Schloss
Wilhelminenberg

Währing

Sandleitengasse

Hernalser Hauptstr.

Lerchenfelder Gürtel

Ottakring

Gablenzgasse

Flötzersteig

Penzing

Rudolfsheim-
Fünfhaus

Neubau

Hütteldorfer

Str.

Neubaugürtel

Linzer

Str.

Hietzinger Kai

Mariahilfer Str.

1

Linke

Schönbrunner

Wienzeile

Schloßstr.

Hietzing

Str.

Maria-
hilf

Schloss
Schönbrunn

Meidling

Lainzer

Eichenstr.

The perfect
overview of Vienna

Wienerbergstr.

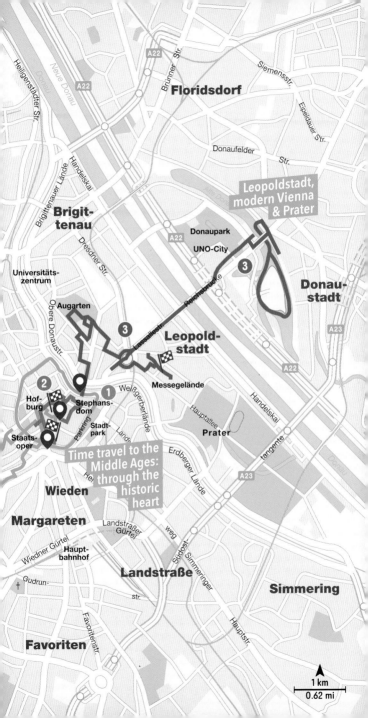

Floridsdorf

Brigit-
tenau

Universitäts-
zentrum

Augarten

Leopoldstadt,
modern Vienna
& Prater

Donaupark

UNO-City

Donau-
stadt

Leopold-
stadt

Messegelände

Prater

Hofburg

Stephans-
dom

Staats-
oper

Stadt-
park

Time travel to the
Middle Ages:
through the
historic
heart

Wieden

Margareten

Haupt-
bahnhof

Landstraßer
Gürtel

Landstraße

Simmering

Favoriten

1 km
0.62 mi

❶ THE PERFECT OVERVIEW OF VIENNA

➤ Magnificent buildings at the Ring: sightseeing by tram
➤ Experience a flagship coffee house and breathtaking art
➤ This is Vienna: Schönbrunn, Stephansdom and Staatsoper

📍 Staatsoper	🏁	Loosbar
→ 20km	🚶	1 day (total walking time 6–7 hours)

ℹ Both the start and end points are connected to public transport, so no need for a car!
On weekdays the last underground trains and trams depart between 11.30pm and 12.30am; they run continuously throughout the weekend. There are also night-time bus services.
Staatsoper: It is best to book tickets in advance!

CIRCLING THE RING BY TRAM

❶ Staatsoper

❷ Ringstrasse

It's a good idea to make an early start to *catch the Line 1 tram* before rush hour starts. The stop is located diagonally opposite the ❶ Staatsoper ➤ p. 33, p. 109 – and it's hard to imagine a more beautiful introduction to the splendour of this former Habsburg capital. As you travel down the ❷ Ringstrasse ➤ p. 30 you will see magnificent buildings glowing in the morning light – the twin edifices of the Naturhistorisches Museum and the Kunsthistorisches Museum, the Parliament, the Rathaus, the Burgtheater, the University. A section of the route also runs alongside the Donaukanal. *Change to tram Line 2 at Urania to complete the circle, heading past the Stadtpark.*

FROM A COFFEE HOUSE TO "VIENNA'S BELLY"

❸ Sperl

Now it's time for breakfast at ▐ ❸ Sperl *(daily | Gumpendorfer Str. 11)*, a prime example of a Viennese coffee house located *just a short walk away on the other side of Schillerplatz,* where you can order a *Melange* and a crispy *Kaisersemmel* bread roll with an egg. Once you're done, *walk down Girardigasse* until you reach the  ❹ Naschmarkt ➤ p. 94 – otherwise known as *der Bauch von Wien* ("Vienna's belly") Here you can find heaps of fruit, vegetables and deli products, which taste as good as they look – make sure you stop to sample the wares every now and then.

❹ Naschmarkt

Circling the Ring: a picturesque journey though the city centre by tram

STROLL THROUGH SCHÖNBRUNN PALACE

At the western end of the Naschmarkt you will find *Kettenbrückengasse station*, from where the U4 will take you to ❺ Schönbrunn ➤ p. 64 in just a few minutes. A guided tour through the state rooms of the palace is a must, and make sure you take a stroll through the extensive palace gardens and all the way up to the Gloriette. If you have time you can also make a detour into the Tiergarten ➤ p. 65, which is the oldest zoo in the world.

❺ Schönbrunn

LUNCH IN THE MQ

By now your stomach should be rumbling, so *head back into the city centre (tram 60, then U3 Volkstheater)*, where the Museumsquartier ➤ p. 51 offers countless inviting cafés and restaurants. The stylish ❻ Halle

❻ Halle Café-Restaurant

Café-Restaurant ➤ p. 76 is very affordable, despite its fine cuisine, and is a good place for an alfresco lunch with views over the inner courtyard of the Museumsquartier. Time for a souvenir? Four photographs in black and white on a strip of paper: next to the main entrance you can take an old-fashioned selfie in the photo booth.

INSIDER TIP
Analogue selfie

EXPERIENCE OLD MASTERS & YOUNG ART

After lunch, head over to the ❼ Kunsthistorisches Museum ➤ p. 35 where you can take in one of the most important art collections in Europe. Located just two minutes' walk away *across Museumsplatz and Maria-Theresien-Platz*, its displays include fine works by a whole host of Old Masters. Those who prefer Schiele, Klimt et al should stay in the Museumsquartier and visit the Leopold Museum ➤ p. 52, while fans of contemporary art can try the neighbouring Museum Moderner Kunst ➤ p. 52.

❼ Kunsthistorisches Museum

CHIC SHOPPING

Now it's time for a little shopping. Cross ❽ Heldenplatz ➤ p. 36 and wander *down Stallburggasse and its side streets* until you reach ❾ Kärntner Strasse. But be warned: the many fashion and handicraft boutiques you'll find here could put your holiday budget in serious jeopardy!

❽ Heldenplatz

❾ Kärntner Strasse

DOWN TO THE CATACOMBS & UP TO THE TOWER

Are you ready for Vienna's number one landmark? The ❿ Stephansdom ➤ p. 44 is a Gothic masterpiece both inside and out, and is well worth exploring in depth. Head down into the catacombs, or for a more uplifting experience, climb the south tower and take in the marvellous views. The city panorama from the terrace of the north tower (accessible by lift) is equally superb.

❿ Stephansdom

BAROQUE SPENDOUR & A MARVELLOUS CAFÉ

You will come across more churches as you wander *north-west towards Schottenring via Graben, Hof and Freyung* – including the Baroque ⓫ Peterskirche with

⓫ Peterskirche

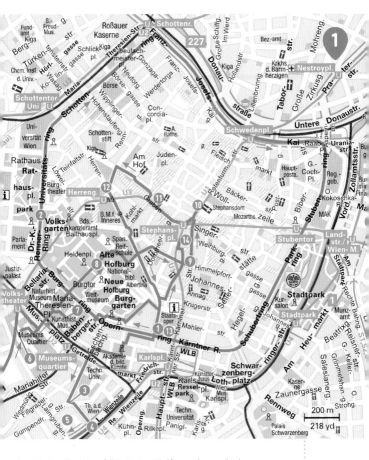

its gloriously colourful interior. Halfway along, duck into the shopping arcade at ⑫ **Palais Ferstel** ➤ p. 46. where you can have dinner at Café Central ➤ p. 74.

TO THE OPERA OR THE THEATRE?

The musically inclined can now head over to the ⑬ Staatsoper ➤ p. 33, 109 which you can reach *in just a few minutes via Herrengasse and Augustinerstrasse.* Alternatively, if you'd rather have a night at the theatre, you can pick up some tickets for the renowned Burgtheater ➤ p. 40, p. 110 or its offshoot, the Akademietheater ➤ p. 110.

⑫ **Palais Ferstel**

⑬ **Staatsoper**

NIGHTLIFE: ART DECO BAR & A TOP CLUB

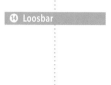

At ⑭ Loosbar ➤ p. 103 (accessible *via Kärntner Strasse across the way from Weihburggasse*), aesthetes can enjoy good drinks and authentic Art Deco style until early morning. If you'd prefer somewhere livelier, with a hip atmosphere and top-name DJs, then head to Passage ➤ p. 105 underneath the Ringstrasse instead.

❷ TIME TRAVEL TO THE MIDDLE AGES: THROUGH THE HISTORIC HEART

➤ Ancient churches, winding alleyways, dreamy courtyards
➤ Hofburg and Heldenplatz: discover the home of the Habsburgs
➤ Stroll through the Sisi Museum and feast on Sachertorte

📍 Stephansdom	🏁	Café Sacher
→ 7km	🚶	6-7 hours (total walking time 1½-2 hours)
ℹ️ You may need to queue for a table at **Café Sacher.**		

STEPHANSDOM & SCHATZKAMMER

The tour starts at Vienna's sacred centre point and its most famous landmark: the ❶ Stephansdom ➤ p. 44. You can visit the nave for free, but also climb the 343 steps of the south tower (5.50 euros) or take the lift to the north tower (6 euros).

Once you have duly admired this filigree sandstone masterpiece, head south-east from the church, *where after a short distance you will reach Singerstrasse.* Here, art lovers should pay a visit to the ❷ Schatzkammer des Deutschen Ordens (Treasury of the Teutonic Knights) *(Mon–Sat 1pm–4pm | admission 5 euros)* at no. 7, with its collection of measuring instruments, precious liturgical vessels and weapons.

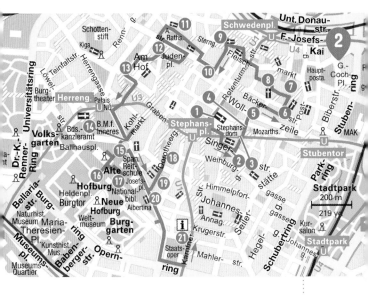

WIENER BLUT (VIENNESE BLOOD) & MOZART

At the next corner, turn left onto ❸ *Blutgasse* – an immaculately restored quarter with cobbled streets, ancient buildings and many a secluded inner courtyard. The ❹ Mozarthaus ➤ p. 50 at the end of the street is where Mozart composed *The Marriage of Figaro* and other masterpieces, and is well worth a look.

❸ Blutgasse

❹ Mozarthaus

CAKE & CHURCHES

Continue down narrow lanes and *across Schulerstrasse until you reach Wollzeile.* If in need of some caffeine, ❺ Café Diglas (*Mon–Sat 8am–10pm, Sun 9am–10pm | Wollzeile 10*) offers a pleasant venue for a cup of coffee, as well as a large selection of delicious cakes. Once refreshed, continue a few steps further *onto Bäcker-strasse and head east past its many picturesque historical façades until you reach Dr-Ignaz-Seipel-Platz,* one of the most impressive squares in the entire city. The double-towered early Baroque façade on its northern end belongs to the ❻ Jesuitenkirche ➤ p. 50; don't miss its mind-blowing *trompe l'oeil* interior ceiling painting – a High Baroque masterpiece by the Italian painter Andrea Pozzo. The magnificent building to the left of the

❺ Café Diglas

❻ Jesuitenkirche

church is the auditorium of the Old University, now home to the Austrian Academy of Sciences.

FROM COURTYARD OASIS TO BERMUDA TRIANGLE

Next, walk part-way down Sonnenfelsgasse before turning right onto the remarkably crooked **❼ Schönlaterngasse**. At house no.7 a strange stone beast commemorates the well-known legend of the basilisk (a mythological reptile) who is reputed to have inhabited the well in the rear courtyard at the start of the 13th century and terrorised the populace. A passageway next door at no. 5 leads onto **❽ Heiligenkreuzer Hof**. Pass through this atmospheric oasis of calm via the gateway opposite and then *turn right and right again. Head west down Fleischmarkt, crossing Rotenturmstrasse*, until you reach the so-called Bermuda Triangle – a lively quarter that is home to many bars and Beisl restaurants. Here, amid all the hustle and bustle, stands one of the oldest churches in the city and a beacon of timeless calm: the Romanesque **❾ Ruprechtskirche ➤ p. 49**.

GOTHIC, BAROQUE & EXCLUSIVE SHOPS

Continue down Judengasse – a mini mecca for followers of fashion with its many boutiques – until you reach **❿ Hoher Markt ➤ p. 48**. Take a short *detour down Salvatorgasse* to visit the church of **⓫ Maria am Gestade ➤ p. 47**, a Gothic jewel crowned with a filigree tower that is unfairly neglected by tourists. Once back on the path, *head past two magnificent Baroque buildings* – the former Bohemian Court Chancellery and the Old City Hall – and on to Judenplatz. Now is an appropriate moment to reflect on the tragic history of Vienna's Jewish community as you are standing in front of the **⓬ Memorial to the Austrian Jewish Victims of the Holocaust**, which takes the form of a stone library. Head *through Drahtgasse* to the next square, **⓭ Am Hof ➤ p. 46**. Just as historically significant as Judenplatz, it was the largest open space in medieval Vienna. The magnificent bank building on its eastern end was converted in 2014 into a spectacular five-star hotel, the

❼ Schönlaterngasse

❽ Heiligenkreuzer Hof

❾ Ruprechtskirche

❿ Hoher Markt
⓫ Maria am Gestade

⓬ Memorial to the Austrian Jewish Victims of the Holocaust

⓭ Am Hof

Look up to the muscular chap who supports the Bohemian Court Chancellery with ease!

Park Hyatt, and behind this you can find the Golden Quarter, a long line of luxury boutiques representing the international fashion and accessories industry.

LOOSHAUS: AN ARCHITECTURAL MILESTONE

Next, *cross Naglergasse and Wallnerstrasse* and head towards ⑭ Michaelerplatz. At the centre of this square archaeologists have uncovered the remains of a Roman house, while at its northern end stands the Looshaus ➤ p. 39. Designed by Adolf Loos and built shortly before World War I, this building's unadorned façade was heavily criticised at first, but is now considered a milestone of modern architecture. A number of years ago the building was painstakingly restored to its original appearance by a local bank, and the simple elegance of its marble façade and wood-panelled foyer have impressed visitors ever since.

⑭ Michaelerplatz

FROM THE SHOPPING MILE TO THE HOFBURG

If at this point you feel like a little window shopping, then you have the perfect venue close at hand in the form of Kohlmarkt, Vienna's most elegant commercial street. However, our tour continues in the opposite direction through the ⑮ Hofburg ➤ p. 36. Start by *passing*

⑮ Hofburg

131

under the Michaelertor gate, with its impressive verdigris dome, and into the inner courtyard. On your right (in the so-called Imperial Chancellery Wing) you can find the entrance to the Kaiserappartements ➤ p. 39, the working rooms and private chambers of Emperor Franz Joseph and his consort Elisabeth, to whom an entire museum is dedicated (the Sisi Museum ➤ p. 39). The same entrance leads to the silver collection Silberkammer ➤ p. 39 which is also well worth a look.

HABSBURGS' FEUDAL SPLENDOUR

Head through the shopping arcade at the south-eastern corner of the courtyard to find yourself on ⑯ Heldenplatz ➤ p. 36, an enormous open area that immerses visitors in all the feudal splendour of the former Habsburg empire. No doubt you will be in need of some lunch by now, and you can find tasty and good-value fare at the ⑰ Green Door Bistro ➤ p. 83 *(entrance behind the Burgkapelle). Afterwards, head south-east off Heldenplatz, past the Michaelerkirche, and continue down Augustinerstrasse. A 250-m detour to the left down Dorotheergasse* will take you to the ⑱ Jewish Museum ➤ p. 44, which hosts a regular programme of extremely interesting themed exhibitions. Afterwards, take a look at the reliably luxurious wares on display in the ⑲ Dorotheum auction house ➤ p. 91 before calling at the Gothic ⑳ Augustinerkirche ➤ p. 34, where members of the Habsburg dynasty would traditionally marry. Then wander *back onto Augustinerstrasse, continuing past the* Albertina ➤ p. 33 and Alfred Hrdlicka's impressive Memorial against War and Fascism ➤ p. 34, until you reach the Staatsoper ➤ p. 33, p. 109

AEINE SACHERTORTE, BITTE!

Here, just behind this world-renowned temple of music, our tour ends in a culinary crescendo at ⚑ ㉑ Café Sacher Wien *(daily 8am–10pm | Philharmonikerstr. 4).* This traditional café bears the same name as the luxury hotel whose ground floor it inhabits, and is the perfect place to enjoy a *Melange* coffee and a piece of the legendary chocolate cake.

⑯ Heldenplatz

⑰ Green Door Bistro

⑱ Jewish Museum

⑲ Dorotheum
⑳ Augustinerkirche

㉑ Café Sacher Wien

❸ LEOPOLDSTADT, MODERN VIENNA & PRATER

➤ Through the Jewish quarter to Baroque gardens
➤ Boating on the Old Danube with a view of the DC Tower
➤ Giant Ferris Wheel and candy floss – pure pleasure!

📍 Schwedenplatz

→ approx. 5km (without U-Bahn journeys)

🏁 Schweizerhaus

🚶 1 day (total walking time 1–2 hours)

ℹ️ This tour is best enjoyed during the summer, as many of its activities are not possible at other times of year.

JEWISH LIFE & TRENDY RESTAURANTS

This city walk starts on the Donaukanal, or more specifically on ❶ Schwedenplatz, and *leads across the bridge bearing the same name into the 2nd District* of Leopoldstadt ➤ p. 58. This warren of small streets was for centuries a ghetto, and was referred to colloquially as Mazzesinsel ("Matzo Island") as it was mainly inhabited by the city's Jewish community prior to 1938. During the Third Reich it was depopulated and "Aryanised", but nowadays it is once again home to a thriving Jewish community with plenty of synagogues, kosher shops and cafés, schools and retirement homes.

❶ Schwedenplatz

Your first stop here is ❷ Karmelitermarkt, *which you get to by heading down the street of the same name that branches left off Taborstrasse (follow the green sign).* This market dates back to 1671, and in recent years has become the centre of a youthful artistic and creative scene. Alongside the traditional food stands you can find a whole host of trendy stores and venues to browse and explore. We recommend stopping at Kaas am Markt *(Mon 8am–3pm, Tue–Fri 8am–6pm, Sat 8am–2pm | stall 33–36),* for a coffee and a pastry or cake. This place is halfway between a delicatessen and a café, and

❷ Karmelitermarkt

offers superb organic and slow-food products as well as delicious small plates.

BAROQUE GARDEN FOR PORCELAIN LOVERS

Head three or four blocks north along Grosse Sperlgasse, and you will find yourself at the entrance to the ❸ Augarten, the oldest preserved Baroque park in all Austria. The former Imperial summer palace of the same name was built here at the end of the 17th century, and is now home to the world-renowned Augarten ➤ p. 93. It's well worth booking a guided tour of the works *(Mon–Thu 10.15am & 11.30am, Thu also 2pm & 3.30pm)* and afterwards visiting the museum and shop to learn about the history of this "white gold" right up to the present day. The stately villa next door is home to the legendary Vienna Boys' Choir, which gives regular concerts in the ultra-modern *Konzertsaal für Musik und Theater (MuTh)* ➤ p. 109. Not a bad way to spend one of your evenings in Vienna!

❸ Augarten

Augarten: admire the porcelain and stroll through the park

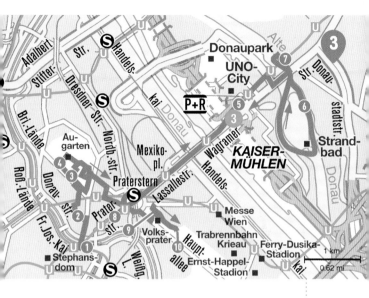

FROM PARK TO UNO-CITY

Hungry yet? During the summer, the garden of the
④ Schankwirtschaft *(Mon–Sun 10am–10pm | Obere*
Augartenstr. 1a | schankwirtschaft.at | €€) at the south-
ern end of the park is a great place to sit and enjoy
some delicious food; if it's cold and rainy, then the
trendy café Schöne Perle *(Mon–Fri from 11am, Sat/Sun*
from 10am | Grosse Pfarrgasse 2 | €€) located one block
to the south, or the offerings at the Karmelitermarkt, are
good alternatives. Walk off your lunch with a stroll
through the leafy avenues of the park, before *heading*
down Novaragasse to Praterstern, from where you can
take the U1 to Kaisermüh-len-VIC station. Your destination is the ⑤ Uno-City – a huge complex consisting of
four glass towers that was opened in 1979, turning
Vienna into the site of the third United Nations office in
the world at that time, and lending a significant international flavour to the city. A 60-minute guided tour
(normally Mon–Fri 11am, 2pm & 3.30pm | admission
15 euros | book online at unis.unvienna.org) will inform
you on the history of the UN and its agencies based in
Vienna, such as the Office on Drugs and Crime and the
International Atomic Energy Agency.

④ Schankwirtschaft

⑤ Uno-City

BOATING ON THE OLD DANUBE

By now your head is probably spinning, so it's time to get some fresh air. The best way to do that during the summer is by taking a relaxing boat trip on the nearby

⑥ Alte Donau (Old Danube) ➤ p. 115 where you will be able to see the impressive skyscraper district of "New Vienna", crowned by the 250m-tall DC Tower. Pedalos and electric boats can be hired from Marina Hofbauer next to the Alte Donau U-Bahn station, or from the sailing school on the opposite bank that goes by the same name. If you would like something more unusual, take to the water in the "island boat", with its very own palm tree *(up to 8 people, 65 euros/hr),* or the "sofa boat" *(for up to 4 people, 49 euros/hr).* It is best to book in advance at Meine-Insel-Bootsvermietung *(meine-insel.at).* Afterwards, stretch your legs a little by strolling along the picturesque shoreline promenade that runs alongside this 8km-long former branch of the Danube, before stopping for a break at the ⑦ Ufertaverne *(daily April noon–9pm, May–Aug 9am–midnight, Sept 9am–9pm, closed in winter | An der Oberen Alten Donau 186 | ufertaverne.at | €)* on the north bank close to the Kagraner Brücke bridge.

⑥ Old Danube

⑦ Ufertaverne

INSIDER TIP
Robinson Crusoe, I presume?

JEWISH VIENNA

Vienna's history is more closely interwoven with that of its Jewish community than almost any other major city in Europe. As early as 1420, hundreds of the city's Jews were driven to collective suicide during the particularly bloody pogrom known as the Vienna Gesera. After the revolution of 1848, the local community experienced a period of tolerance and its population grew to 200,000, making it one of the largest and most vibrant in Europe.

However, after the annexation of Austria in 1938, around a third of the city's Jewish inhabitants were murdered in concentration camps by the Nazis, while the rest were forced to flee. Very few survived going underground in the city. Nowadays, Vienna is home to around 15,000 Jews.

You need a head for heights to appreciate Vienna from the Giant Ferris Wheel

KING OF THE WALTZ & GIANT FERRIS WHEEL

For the last stage of the tour, *take the U1 back to Praterstern. At no. 54 Praterstrasse* you can visit the ⑧ Strauss Memorial *(Tue–Sun 10am–1pm & 2–6pm | admission 5 euros)*, the apartment where waltz-wunderkind Johann Strauss the Younger lived for many years and composed countless works, including "The Blue Danube". His vivacious spirit is well expressed by the next stop on the tour: the ⑨ Riesenrad ➤ p. 60. A ride in one of the red wooden cars of the Giant Ferris Wheel takes visitors up to lofty heights for an unusual perspective. Afterwards, *explore the Volksprater amusement park at the foot of this steel landmark*, where you can win a rose for the love of your life at the shooting arcade, or take them for a head-spinning, stomach-churning roller-coaster ride. For a calmer, more child-friendly option, take a 20-minute trip through the woods on the 🎭 Liliputbahn miniature railway *(July/Aug 10am–7.30pm, May/ June 10am–7pm, April, Sept 10am–6pm, March, Oct 10am–5pm | ticket 5 euros | entrance behind the planetarium).*

⑧ Strauss Memorial

⑨ Riesenrad

HEARTY FOOD OR DANCING THE NIGHT AWAY?

 Schweizerhaus

Round off your tour with a culinary experience that is as authentic as it is substantial at the ⑩ Schweizerhaus ➤ p. 84. Not ready to go home yet? If you're up for a dance and don't mind getting up close and personal with your fellow partygoers, then head to the *Praterdome* ➤ p.105, Austria's biggest disco.

④ KAHLENBERG & LEOPOLDSBERG

➤ Relaxed hiking through vineyards
➤ Enjoy Vienna from a height: cosy taverns with great views
➤ Lie in the grass, dream and listen to the music

📍 Grinzing	🏁 Grinzing
🔄 approx. 10km (without bus journeys)	🥾 4–6 hours (total walking time 2½–3 hours)
📶 Very easy	↗ approx. 300m
ℹ There's no need to rush for the return trip to Grinzing – bus no. 38A departs every 15 mins until midnight.	

STARTING POINT: GRINZING

Anyone looking to scale Vienna's local hills on foot should buy a 24-hour ticket for 8 euros and *take tram 38 to its terminus, or bus 38A to the stop* ① Grinzing. From here, *head north up the gentle slope of Grinzinger Steig* until you reach the atmospheric cemetery at ② Heiligenstädter Friedhof. *Continue due west along the Schreiberbach stream, slowly climbing the Mukental valley.*

① Grinzing

650m 13 mins

② Heiligenstädter Friedhof

PAST VINEYARDS & MEADOWS

The at times open and sunny, at times shaded, path you are walking along is called the *Wildgrubgasse*. Its start is lined by several *Heuriger* taverns, but the atmosphere soon grows more rural, and you'll be surrounded

A lovely evening: your long ascent to the Kahlenberg is rewarded with a *Heuriger*

by open meadows interspersed with picturesque vine-yards. You will *walk past the vineyard belonging to the Club der Grinzinger*, where countless celebrities from across the world – from Bill Clinton and Mikhail Gorbachev to Sophia Loren and Udo Jürgens – have adopted their own vine. Inside a gorge on your left there is also an eye-catching (and clearly hand-built) treehouse. The tarmac later gives way to a dirt track that runs through a timber forest over intermittently loamy soil. Finally, *turn right (following a sign)* to access the largely traffic-free Kahlenberger Strasse, which winds its way to the top of the ❸ Kahlenberg.

3km 70 mins

❸ Kahlenberg

PUT YOUR FEET UP

Atop this imposing 484m-high forested hill, the Café Kahlenberg *(March–Oct daily 7am–11pm, Nov–Feb daily 7am–9pm | Am Kahlenberg 3a)* entices visitors with delicious desserts and organic coffee. With a total of three terraces (which in summer are furnished with loungers) and a winter garden, it offers splendid views of Vienna in all its glory.

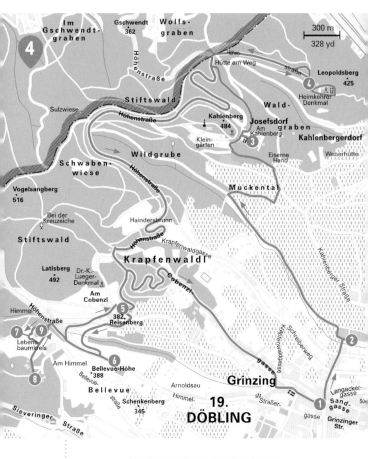

DETOUR TO THE LEOPOLDSBERG

1.7km   26 mins

❹ Leopoldsberg

After a brief visit to the neighbouring Josephskirche, church – built in 1683 as a monument to the battle that began here between a Christian army and the Turkish besiegers of Vienna – *continue along a wide footpath* which in less than half an hour takes you to the top of ❹ Leopoldsberg. Here, you find ruins of the mighty fortress built in the 13th century by the Babenberger dynasty and the recently renovated, double-towered Leopoldskirche church. The path running round the walls of the complex offers magnificent views over the city and its river. You can then take a rest in the Hofgarten.

TO THE MEADOW OF DREAMS

Next, it's worth taking *a short bus trip drive (on the no. 38A) along the panoramic route* to the so-called ⑤ Cobenzl, a look-out point on top of the Kahlenberg. Alternatively, those with more stamina can, of course, head back to the Kahlenberg on foot, from where you can go west along the footpath that borders this panoramic road, which was built during the 1930s as a job creation scheme.

At the end of this walk of just under an hour you will find several attractions. The first is the ⑥ Bellevue-Höhe *close to where Himmelstrasse joins Höhenstrasse*, less than ten minutes' walk from Cobenzl, where a bronze plaque mounted on a stone slab and positioned under a group of trees at the edge of a large meadow commemorates the fact that here, "on 24 July 1895, Dr Sigm. Freud first discovered the secret of dreams".

LISTEN TO THE MUSIC IN THE GRASS

You should also make sure you pay a quick visit to the ⑦ Lebensbaumkreis Am Himmel *(himmel.at)*, a natural monument designed as a sound space, where you can lie back in the grass on weekend afternoons and listen to classical music or jazz played from over 40 speakers while you admire the views across Vienna – all free of charge.

CLOSE TO SISI & TO HEAVEN

Nostalgic culture vultures will also enjoy the nearby neo-Gothic ⑧ Sisi-Kapelle. Afterwards, head over to the nearby ⑨ Oktogon Am Himmel *(April–Oct Fri noon–9.30pm, Sat/Sun 11am–9.30pm, Nov–March Fri noon–9.30pm, Sat/Sun 11am–9.30pm | Himmelstr./ Höhenstr.)*, a café and restaurant housed in a building flooded with light, where you can enjoy coffee and cake or something more substantial as you continue to take in the glorious panoramic views. Finally, *back at Cobenzl, take bus 38A back down into the valley* until you reach ① Grinzing or to the terminus at Heiligenstadt station (on the U4).

6.4km   16 mins

⑤ Cobenzl

900m   13 mins

⑥ Bellevue-Höhe

1km   17 mins

⑦ Lebensbaumkreis Am Himmel

400m   5 mins

⑧ Sisi-Kapelle

500m   7 mins

⑨ Oktogon Am Himmel

3.9km   19 mins

① Grinzing

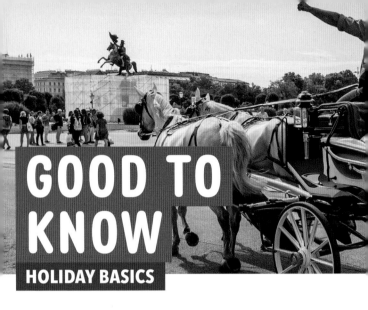

ARRIVAL

ARRIVAL

There are non-stop flights daily to Vienna, operated by British Airways, Austrian, Lufthansa, and other carriers, from airports in the UK and USA. Vienna's International Airport is located in Schwechat, 15km south-east of the city centre.

Since it was opened in 2015, Vienna's enormous new main train station has functioned as a core railway hub for central Europe. All long-distance trains to and from Vienna stop here, including those from Prague and Switzerland, and there are also direct connections to the U-Bahn and tram networks, as well as local and regional services. A 24-hour railway information hotline is available *(tel. 05 17 17)*.

Companies including Flixbus *(flix bus.co.uk)* and Eurolines *(eurolines. de)* can take you from London to Vienna by coach. You'll probably arrive at the Vienna International Busterminal (VIB), right next to the U-Bahn station (U3) Erdberg. A new long-distance coach terminal is currently being built.

CLIMATE & WHEN TO GO

Vienna has a moderate continental climate. This means cold winters, hot, relatively dry summers and rain in spring and autumn. The best time to visit the city is in late spring or early autumn. Weather forecast: *wetter.orf. at.*

The *Fiaker* is Vienna's classic form of transport, especially for tourists

GETTING AROUND

FROM THE AIRPORT INTO THE CITY

There are buses from the airport to the southern (Südbahnhof) and western (Westbahnhof) railway stations *(ticket 9 euro | travel time approx. 30 mins)* as well as the half-hourly Cityairport Train (CAT) to Wien-Mitte *(ticket 14.90 euros | travel time 16 mins | cityairporttrain.com).* A cheap alternative: the S-Bahn (S7) suburban railway runs every half hour to Wien Mitte or Praterstern station *(4.30 euros, half price with the Vienna City Card | travel time approx. 25 mins).* Tickets are available at the red ÖBB ticket machines and *NOT* at the green CAT machines!

INSIDER TIP
Arrive like the Viennese

If you want to take a taxi *(to the city centre from approx. 36 euros | travel time approx. 25 mins)*, make sure that you don't take one of the ones parked directly outside the airport because these are much more expensive as they cross from one federal state into another! Use the 40 100 taxi rank in the reception hall instead.

DRIVING

The traffic regulations in Austria are similar to those in most other European countries. It is compulsory for drivers to wear seatbelts and have high visibility jackets in the car in the case of a breakdown; winter tyres are obligatory from November to March and motorcyclists must wear a helmet. The legal drink-driving limit is 0.5%. The speed limit on motorways is 130kmh, on main roads 100kmh and 50kmh in built up areas. Breakdown assistance: ÖAMTC (tel. 120) and ARBÖ (tel. 123).

E-scooters: a modern alternative to the *Fiaker*

hr | book at Fiaker Susi tel. 0699 10 60 29 35). Riding Dinner (riding-dinner.com) offers culinary *Fiaker* rides for one to four people.

BICYCLE AND E-SCOOTER HIRE

You can hire one of 3,000 "WienMobil" bicycles *(0.60 euro/30 mins, see the Wien-Mobil app for locations)* around the clock at more than 185 hire stations. Cycling paths are well signposted. E-scooters, which can be found everywhere in the city, are hired out by various operators. You are charged per minute on the road, and the locations are shown in the apps *(li. me, bird.co, tier.app)*.

PUBLIC TRANSPORT

Vienna has five U-Bahn (underground) lines (operating approx. 5am–12.30am with 24-hour service on the nights before Saturday, Sunday and public holidays), as well as several suburban railway lines (S-Bahn) and countless tram, bus and night-bus lines. A sixth underground line (confusingly called the U5 because the U6 already exists) is currently under construction. At the time of writing, the U2 section between Schottentor and Karlsplatz was still closed.

For information about the fastest route to your destination see the WienMobil app by Wiener Linien. All tickets can be purchased at machines at U-Bahn stations; tickets for the night bus can be bought on the bus. A single ticket for bus, underground, tram or suburban railway (within the city borders) costs 2.40 euros. The Klimakarte *(a day-ticket for the entire*

During the day, parking is only allowed for 120 minutes at a time with a parking disc in most Viennese districts, available from newsagents. Better to park in a 🚗 park-and-ride multistorey *(3.60 euros/day | parkand ride.at)* at an underground terminus and go to the centre on the U-Bahn.

FIAKER

Sitting comfortably in a horse-drawn carriage is a stylish way to become acquainted with the beauty of Vienna. A big city tour (approx. 40 mins) costs 95 euros; a 20-minute tour is 55 euros. All of the *Fiaker* ranks are in the 1st District: on Augustinerstrasse in front of the Albertina *(🗺 b7)*, on Heldenplatz at the outer Burgtor *(🗺 b7)*, on Michaelerplatz *(🗺 b7)* and on Stephansplatz at the cathedral's north side *(🗺 c6)*, in front of Petersplatz *(🗺 b–c6)* and outside the Burgtheater *(🗺 a6)*. Special carriages available with wheelchair access *(130 euros | 1*

network, valid on eight separate days) costs 40.80 euros, and there are even cheaper network tickets for 24 hours (8 euros), 48 hours (14.10 euros) or 72 hours (17.10 euros) as well as the 🐷 Wochenkarte, valid from Monday–Monday (17.10 euros).

All of the above tickets are valid within the entire city area – in Vienna there are no zones as you may know them from other major cities. Information for excursions by train in the immediate area of Vienna is available 24 hours on tel. 0 51 71 73 as well as at oebb.at and on the ÖBB Scotty app. Visitors to the city may purchase the 24-, 48- or 72-hour Vienna City Card (see p. 148) and EasyCityPass (15, 20 and 25 euros respectively | easycitypass.com). These tickets are valid for one adult plus one child under 15 and they include various discounts to museums and sights. There is also an Erlebnisticket (experience ticket) for LGBTIQ visitors. For up-to-date travel information visit wienerlinien.at.

In general, children under six travel free of charge, as do those up to 15 on Sundays and public holidays, and during school breaks (ID required!). There are discounted tickets for children (aged 6–15) and pensioners (from age 65) as well as for dogs, which are only allowed on public transport on a lead and with a muzzle.

There are lifts in most underground stations and almost all vehicles have lowered doors and sufficient space for pushchairs, etc. The transport fleet consists mainly of low-level vehicles without steps. Station displays announce those trams which are suited for wheelchair users. For general info about wheelchair-friendly infrastructure visit wien.info/de/reiseinfos/wien-barrierefrei.

TAXIS

Radio taxis tel. 01 3 13 00, 01 401 00, 01 60160, or 01 8 14 00. Basic fee on workdays: 3.40 euros; Sunday 3.80 euros, order via radio an additional 2 euros. Fares for journeys outside the city limits should be agreed on in advance.

EMERGENCIES

CONSULATES & EMBASSIES
BRITISH EMBASSY
Jauresgasse 12 | 1030 Vienna | tel. +43 1 71 6130 | viennaconsular enquiries@fco.gov.uk

U.S. EMBASSY
Boltzmanngasse 16 | 1090 Vienna | tel. +43 1 313390 | austria.usembassy. gov

CANADIAN EMBASSY
Laurenzerberg 2 | 1010 Vienna | tel. +43 15 31 38 3000 | canadainter national.gc.ca/austria-autriche

EMERGENCY NUMBERS
24-hour chemists: tel. 14 55
Emergency doctor: tel. 141
Fire brigade: tel. 122
Police: tel. 133
Ambulance: tel. 144
Night dentist: tel. 01 5 12 2078

ESSENTIALS

BANKS & CREDIT CARDS

Major credit cards are accepted in most places. Reports of loss and queries: *American Express tel. 01 51 5110, Diners Club tel. 01 50 13 50, MasterCard tel. 01 717010, Visa tel. 01 7 11 11.*

CITY TOURS & WALKS

By tram: circling the Ringstrasse on the Ring Tram. For up-to-date information visit *wien.info*. It is cheaper to take trams 1 and 2, which run along the same route; you only need to buy a public transport ticket (2.40 euros).

INSIDER TIP
Cheaper by tram

On four wheels: in a chauffeured vintage car through the city and out into the countryside ith Oldiefahrt *(tel. 06 64 4 11 88 93 | oldiefahrt.at).* Private hour-long tours in a vintage car at *oldtimertours.at.*

On two wheels: guided bicycle tours lasting 2–3 hours with *Bike & Guide (tel. 06 6 45 16 35 33 | bikeandguide.com), Pedal Power (tel. 01 7 29 72 34 | pedalpower.at), Vienna Explorer (viennaexplorer.com)* and *Prime Tours (primetours.at).* A free Vienna bicycle map, the *Radkarte Wien,* is available at *Wien Hotels & Info (tel. 01 2 45 55);* otherwise the bookshop *Freytag & Berndt (Wallnerstrasse 3)* has the best maps.

By bus: *Vienna Sightseeing Tours (24-hr ticket for 4 routes 32 euros online | tel. 01 71 246830 | viennasightseeing.at)* and *Big Bus Vienna (day-ticket for 2 routes 35 euros online | tel. 01 90 59 10 00 | bigbustours.com/de)* organise several tours of the city every day. The hop-on-hop-off buses run on fixed routes between around 50 stations, and you can get on and off as you wish.

By motorboat *(only May–Oct):* DDSG Blue Danube Schifffahrt (tel. 01 58 88 00 | ddsg-blue-danube.at). Their Grosse Donaurundfahrt (big Danube round trip) costs 27.50 euros, and the Abendrundfahrt (evening round trip) 36.50 euros. You can also visit the Slovakian capital Bratislava (single trip 33 euros, at the weekend 38 euros).

On foot: free city walks are offered by *Vienna Greeters (2 hrs, book 2 weeks in advance at vienna greeters.com/willkommen-in-wien)* and *Good Tours (goodviennatours.eu/de).* Donations welcome. The *Vienna Guide Service (tel. 01 5 87 3633 62 | guides-in-vienna.at)* arranges guides for group tours; half a day from 225 euros, full day from around 450 euros.

The charity Wiener Spaziergänge (Vienna walks) provides a selection of licenced tourist guides for city-specific topics (20 euros/person). For monthly schedules see online and ask at tourist information offices *(wienguide.at).*

On any of the numerous inner city or greenbelt tours run by the *Fotofüchse* (photo foxes) *(from 99 euros | diefotofuechse.com)* you will be accompanied by two professional photographers.

To be introduced to Vienna by refugees and (formerly)

INSIDER TIP
See Vienna with new eyes

homeless people for a cliché-free view of the city, book a tour with *Shades Tours (from 18 euros | shades-tours.com)* and the *Backstreet Guides (17 euros | backstreet-guides.at).*

If you find walking too slow, book a sporty sightseeing tour where you jog past the sights, for example with *Vienna SightRunning (vienna-sightrunning.at)*, Ruth Riehle – Run and See (*ruthriehle.at*) or *Go! Running Tours Vienna (gorunningtoursvienna.com).*

CUSTOMS

For government limits on quantities of alcohol, tobacco and other goods that that can be brought into the UK, see *gov.uk*. For US regulations, see *cbp.gov*.

INTERNET ACCESS & WIFI

Many cafés and institutions provide free WiFi. You can download a list of the more than 600 hotspots at *freewave.at*. The city of Vienna also offers public WiFi in more than 400 locations (see the Stadt Wien live app).

POST

Opening times usually *Mon–Fri 8am–noon and 2pm–6pm (cash desks to 5pm)*; main district post offices *(Mon–Fri 8am–6pm, Sat 9am–noon)*; main post office *(Mon–Fri 8am–7pm, Sat 10am–6pm | Fleischmarkt 19 | U4 Schwedenplatz | ⬜ d6)*; Westbahnhof *(Mon–Fri 8am–7pm, Sat 9am–6pm | Europaplatz 3 | U3, U6 Westbahnhof | ⬜ G10)*. Info: tel. 08 10 01 01 00

PUBLIC HOLIDAYS

1 Jan	New Year's Day
6 Jan	Epiphany
March/April	Easter Monday
1 May	Labour Day
May	Ascension Day
May/June	Whit Monday
May/June	Corpus Christi
15 Aug	Assumption Day
26 Oct	National Day
1 Nov	All Saints' Day
8 Dec	Feast of the Immaculate Conception
25/26 Dec	Christmas

SMOKING

Austria has long remained an outpost of the smoking fraternity, but now the country's catering and hotel industries all observe legal smoking bans. Some hotels (those without restaurants) have separate smoking rooms.

TELEPHONE & MOBILE

Check with your provider whether your UK mobile is still able to use roaming without extra charge post-Brexit.

Making telephone calls within Austria is cheap. If you intend to stay in the country for a long time, it is worth buying a prepaid card from the main operators: *A 1 (a1.net)*, *Orange (orange.at)*, *T-Mobile (t-mobile.at)*, *Hutchison 3 (drei.at)*. Their networks are used by ⬱ budget providers such as *hot (hot.at)*, *yesss (yesss.at)* or *spusu (spusu.at)*. SIM cards and top-ups are available at supermarkets, newsagents *(Trafik)* and post office branches.

The international dialling code for Austria is *0043*, the area code for Vienna *(0)1*. Dial *00 44* for the UK, followed by the area code without the 0, and 001 for the USA and Canada.

THEATRE & CONCERT TICKETS

Ticket sales for the Staatsoper for the following season start from April/May. Advance tickets for the Staatsoper, Volksoper, Burgtheater and Akademietheater, as well as last-minute tickets, are available at the Bundestheater box office *(Operngasse 2 | bundestheater. at)*, online at *culturall.com* and with a credit card on *tel. 01 5 13 15 13*. Information on *tel. 01 5 14 44 78 80* or at *ticketinfo@artforart.at.*

Wien-Ticket is the organisation responsible for tickets to the Theater an der Wien, Ronacher, Raimundtheater and all other WVS venues. *Central box office: Wien-Ticket Pavilion (daily 10am–7pm | next to the Opera | bookings by credit card (9am–9pm) tel. 01 5 88 85 | wien-ticket.at).*

Tickets on the internet: *culturall. com* and *viennaticketoffice.com*.

TIPPING

It's usual to tip waiters and taxi drivers between 5 and 10 per cent: room service and porters naturally appreciate a tip as well.

TOURIST INFORMATION

General information is available from *Wien-Tourismus* in the city centre *(daily 9am–6pm | Albertinaplatz | Maysedergasse | tel. 01 2 45 55 | ⌕ b7)* as well as in the airport's arrival hall *(daily 9am–6pm | wien.info).*

Information, advice and tickets for visitors up to age 26 are available at *Jugend-Info (Mon–Fri 2.30–6.30pm*

| Babenbergerstr. | Burgring | tel. 01 4 00 08 41 00 | jugendinfowien.at | ⌕ b8) or *Kinder-Info (Tue–Fri 2–6pm, Sat/Sun 10am–5pm | im Museumsquartier/Hof | tel. 01 4 00 08 44 00 | kinderinfowien.at | ⌕ a8).*

VIENNA CITY CARD

The *Vienna City Card* entitles holders to unlimited use of public transport within the city boundaries for 24, 48 or 72 hours (17, 25 and 29 euros respectively), with one child up to age 15 included for free. It also gives reductions on entry to most museums and sights. In addition, the *Vienna City Card Transfer* offers free transfer from and to Vienna airport by any means of public transport, including check-in at the CAT station Wien Mitte/Landstrasse (34, 42 and 46 euros respectively), with up to two children included. A hop-on-hop-off bus tour and a guided city walk are additions that come with the *Vienna City Card Tour* (44, 52 and 56 euros respectively). The *Vienna City Card Transfer+Tour* comprises not just the bus tour but also the airport transfer (61, 69 and 73 euros respectively). ID required! The above four variations of the card are available online *(vienna citycard.at)*, at the airport, in many hotels, from the tourist information offices on the Albertinaplatz *(daily 9am–6pm)* and at the Hauptbahnhof *(daily 9am–7pm)*, at all ÖBB ticket offices and at the larger sales offices of the Wiener Verkehrslinien *(for example, at Hauptbahnhof, Karlsplatz/ Passage and Westbahnhof | Mon–Fri 6.30am–7pm, Sat 9am–4pm | tel. 01 7 90 91 00 | wienerlinien.at).*

Use the Vienna City Card to get around on the tram network

WEATHER IN VIENNA

	JAN	FEB	MARCH	APRIL	MAY	JUNE	JULY	AUG	SEPT	OCT	NOV	DEC
Daytime temperature	1°	3°	8°	14°	19°	22°	25°	24°	20°	14°	7°	3°
Night-time temperature	-4°	-2°	1°	6°	10°	13°	15°	15°	11°	7°	3°	-1°
☀ Sunshine hours/day	2	3	4	6	7	8	8	8	7	5	2	1
🌧 Rainy days/month	8	7	8	8	9	9	9	9	7	8	8	8

☀ Sunshine hours/day   🌧 Rainy days/month

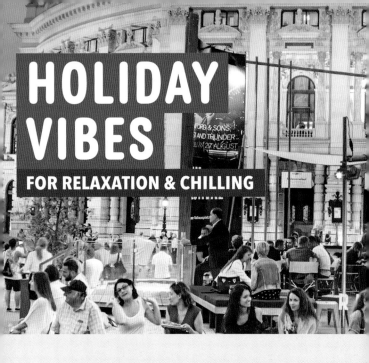

HOLIDAY VIBES
FOR RELAXATION & CHILLING

FOR BOOKWORMS & FILM BUFFS

🎬 MISSION: IMPOSSIBLE – ROGUE NATION
The Austrian chancellor is assassinated in this action thriller where Tom Cruise hunts down the boss of an underground organisation. Highlight: the chase across the roof of the Vienna Staatsoper. (2015)

📖 ES GEHT UNS GUT (WE ARE DOING FINE)
Arno Geiger skilfully links the story of a bourgeois Vienna family with the history of Austria. The novel was awarded the German Book Prize. (2005)

📖 THE STRUDLHOF STEPS
Heimito von Doderer scales literary peaks in his novel on the typical Viennese way of living and thinking in the years shortly before and after World War I. (1951)

🎬 KOMM, SÜSSER TOD (COME SWEET DEATH)
In his role as ex-detective Brenner, star satirist Josef Hader takes the audience to out-of-the-way snack bars, housing blocks on the city's outskirts and the Danube Island Festival in Wolfgang Murnberger's criminal comedy. (2000)

PLAYLIST

0:58

II DER NINO AUS WIEN – PRATERLIED
Wienerlied (traditional Viennese songs) reloaded: humorous vernacular pop.

▶ OSTBAHN-KURTI & DIE CHEFPARTIE – FEUER
Good old-fashioned Austropop (1985), from artists like legendary singer Willi Resetarits. (2022)

▶ GRANADA – WIEN WORT AUF DI
Vernacular cover version of Billy Joel's piano classic "Vienna". (1977)

▶ FALCO – VIENNA CALLING
"Wien, nur Wien, du kennst mich up, kennst mich down" (Vienna, only you know me when I am happy or low) – Austria's musical ambassador Falco (1998) is a must.

▶ BILDERBUCH – BABA
Good pop by one of the most successful local bands.

Your holiday soundtrack can be found on **Spotify** under **MARCO POLO** Vienna

Or scan this code with the Spotify app

GOODNIGHT.AT
Which restaurants and clubs have opened recently? What can I do tonight and at the weekend? Up-to-date news and trends for the coolest events.

WIEN MOBIL
Never again miss your U-Bahn train – with the mobile information service by Wiener Linien, including real-time display, route planner and full network maps. You can also use this app to buy tickets and obtain information about travel disruption.

VIENNAINSIDER.COM
Una and Isidora are sisters, students – and social media experts. They post food and fashion stories about the city, the likes of "The most Instagramable cafés in Vienna".

WIEN.GV.AT/ENGLISH
Comprehensive information on life in the city: leisure, culture, sport, food and drink, sightseeing and much more. The virtual walks make it possible for you to experience all this in the comfort of your own home.

USEFUL WORDS

SMALL TALK

Yes/no/maybe	ja/nein/vielleicht
Please/thank you	bitte/danke
Good morning/afternoon/evening/night	Gute(n) Morgen/Tag!/Nacht!
Hello/Goodbye	Hallo!/Auf Wiedersehen!/
Bye	Tschüss!
My name is ...	Ich heisse ...
What's your name (formal)?	Wie heissen Sie?
Sorry/excuse me	Wie bitte? / Entschuldige!/ Entschuldigen Sie!
I (don't) like this.	Das gefällt mir (nicht).
I would like.../Do you have...?	... istiyorum/... var mı?

EATING & DRINKING

Could I have the menu please?	Die Speisekarte, bitte.
Could I please have ...?	Könnte ich bitte ... haben?
bottle/carafe/glass	Flasche/Karaffe/Glas
knife/fork/spoon	messer/gabel/ löffel
salt/pepper/sugar	salz/pfeffer/zucker
vinegar/oil	essig/öl
milk/cream/lemon	milch/creme/zitrone
fizzy/still water	sprudelwasser/stilles wasser
vegetarian/ allergy	vegetarierin/allergie
Could I have the bill please?	Könnte ich bitte die Rechnung haben.
bill/receipt/tip	rechnung/erhalt/spitze
cash/debit card/credit card	kasse/kreditkarte/debitkarte

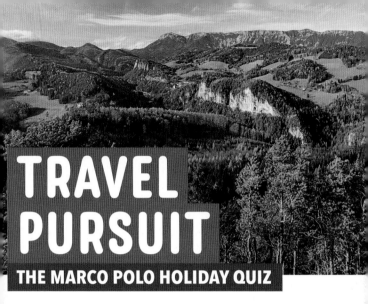

TRAVEL PURSUIT
THE MARCO POLO HOLIDAY QUIZ

Do you know what makes Vienna tick? Test your knowledge of the idiosyncrasies and eccentricities of the city and its people. You'll find the answers at the foot of the page, with more detailed explanations on pages 20 to 25.

❶ Which drug was Empress Sisi addicted to?
a) Cocaine
b) Heroin
c) Cannabis

❷ Which of these creative names has not yet been used by a local band?
a) Voodoo Jürgens
b) 5/8erl in Ehr'n
c) Schau ma mal

❸ Which of the following was invented in Vienna?
a) Schnitzel
b) Goulash
c) none of the above

❹ What do the Viennese call a spritz?
a) Gespritzt
b) Saurer
c) Wiener Mischung

❺ Where does Vienna get its tap water from?
a) From the Rax mountains
b) From the Danube
c) From a spring in the Donauauen National Park

❻ In which year did legendary Austrian singer and musician Falco die in a fatal car crash?
a) 1992
b) 1998
c) 2001

Correct answers: 1a, 2c, 3c, 4a, 5a, 6b

INDEX

WE WANT TO HEAR FROM YOU!

Did you have a great holiday? Is there something on your mind? Whatever it is, let us know! Whether you want to praise the guide, alert us to errors or give us a personal tip – MARCO POLO would be pleased to hear from you. Please contact us by email:

sales@heartwoodpublishing.co.uk

We do everything we can to provide the very latest information for your trip. Nevertheless, despite all of our authors' thorough research, errors can creep in. MARCO POLO does not accept any liability for this.

PICTURE CREDITS
Cover photo: Giant Ferris Wheel, Wurstelprater. (Ekaterina Pokrovsky/Shutterstock.com)
Photos: B. Breitegger (155); DuMont Bildarchiv: T. Anzenberger (10, 17, 31, 98/99, 112/113, 150/151), E. Wrba (9, 70/71, 93); Heidrun Henke (118/119); huber-images: C. Bäck (41), F. Cogoli (12/13), O. Fantuz (6/7), H.-J. Jockschat (111), M. Ripani (14/15), R. Schmid (60, 137); Laif: P. Adenis (48), E. Rois & B. Stubenrauch (106, 120/121, 134), T. Gerber (36/37), R. Haidinger (21), Kirchgessner (97), T. Linkel (26/27), P. Rigaud (83, 85, 86/87, 139), M.-O. Schulz (33), B. Steinhilber (78), C. Stukhard (50); Laif/hemis.fr: L. Maisant (76); Laif/Le Figaro Magazine: Martin (34); Laif/robertharding: E. Rooney (2/3), M. Runkel (44); Look: R. Mirau (69), T. Richter (25); mauritius images / TPG RF (57); mauritius images: W. Dieterich (142/143), W. Dietrich (52), R. Mattes (8), R. Mirau (125), V. Preusser (64, 152); mauritius images/Alamy: I. Dagnall (94/95), K. Thomas (Klappe vorne außen, Klappe vorne innen, 1), E. Wrba (54); mauritius images/Alamy/Alamy Stock Photos (144, R. Babakin (38), I. Dagnall (74), K. Ripak (81); mauritius images/Alamy/RUBI cesartarragona: C. O. Crespo (114/115); mauritius images/Alamy/volkerpreusser (116/117); mauritius images/Alamy/Zoonar/sven h (131); mauritius images/allOver (58); mauritius images/Hemis.fr: B. Gardel (75); mauritius images/imagebroker: K. F. Schöfmann (67); mauritius images/Masterfile R. M.: R. I. Lloyd (108); mauritius images/Westend61: K. Thomas (4); picture-alliance: R. Hackenberg (104); picture-alliance/APA/picturedesk.com: R. Herrgott (91), H. Lehmann (11); picture-alliance/EPA: C. Bruna (22); Stephan Lemke (103); Sergii Figurnyi//Shutterstock.com (149), Chuengjoproduction/Shutterstock.com (156)

3rd Edition - fully revised and updated 2023
Worldwide Distribution: Heartwood Publishing Ltd, Bath, United Kingdom
www.heartwoodpublishing.co.uk

Authors: Benjamin Breitegger, Walter M. Weiss
Editor: Martin Silbermann
Picture editor: Gabriele Forst
Cartography: © MAIRDUMONT, Ostfildern (pp. 122–123, 127, 129, 135, 140, pull-out map); © MAIRDUMONT, Ostfildern, using data from OpenStreetMap, licence CC-BY-SA 2.0 (pp. 28–29, 32, 43, 51, 55, 59, 63, 72–73, 88–89, 100–101)
Cover design and pull-out map cover design: bilekjaeger_Kreativagentur with Zukunftswerkstatt, Stuttgart
Page design: Langenstein Communication GmbH, Ludwigsburg

Heartwood Publishing credits:
Translated from the German by Thomas Moser, Robert Scott McInnes; Jozef van der Voort
Editors: Rosamund Sales, Kate Michell, Felicity Laughton
Prepress: Summerlane Books, Bath
Printed in India

MARCO POLO AUTHOR
BENJAMIN BREITEGGER

Benjamin never wanted to live in a big city, but found himself first in Vienna and later in Hamburg, Berlin and Munich. In the end, the bright Danube Island and the dark *Beisl* pubs were too strong a pull and he returned to the Austrian capital. Today, Benjamin lives in Vienna's Leopoldstadt quarter and works as a journalist for various newspapers and broadcasters.